Golden Words
for
Every Day

Golden Words
for
Every Day

RUTH C. IKERMAN

ABINGDON 🎵 PRESS

NASHVILLE AND NEW YORK

GOLDEN WORDS FOR EVERY DAY

Copyright © 1969 by Abingdon Press

Standard Book Number: 687-15486-3

Library of Congress Catalog Card Number: 69-18457

SET UP, PRINTED, AND BOUND BY THE
PARTHENON PRESS, AT NASHVILLE,
TENNESSEE, UNITED STATES OF AMERICA

Dedicated to

my sister-in-law FLEETA MAE PERCIVAL
with affection and appreciation

Preface

When a friend gave me a white notebook which had a golden pencil attached, it seemed too lovely to use for writing grocery lists or jotting down memos about mending or laundry. This golden pencil became very special in my daily life, as I used it each morning to put down in the notebook a Bible verse which seemed to have pertinent meaning for the day ahead.

Over the years the pencil with the golden lead has helped me find strength for facing problems, and has increased the joy of the happy things which happen through busy routine days. It is in my heart to share this spiritual notebook with other busy women.

Here is a Bible verse for each day of the year, followed by a paragraph of comment and a sentence or two of prayer. Perhaps this material may help us all to frame our own prayers for strength to meet the demands of the space age, and for ultimate peace in the world. May there be a golden halo of faith and trust around your home and in your heart as you use these *Golden Words for Every Day*.

RUTH C. IKERMAN

January

DEAR GOD, WE ARE GRATEFUL FOR
THE PRIVILEGE OF LIVING IN THIS
FIRST MONTH OF THE NEW YEAR.
HELP US HOLD FIRMLY TO THE HIGH
RESOLVES MADE TO SERVE THEE
BETTER.

JANUARY 1. *Choose you this day whom ye will serve
. . . but as for me and my house, we will serve the
Lord.*—JOSHUA 24:15

One of the first decisions of each new year is selecting
the calendar to hang on the kitchen or den wall, where
family activities may be recorded. Do we want the
calendar with the picture of the adorable baby lying in
the crib, or of boys and girls wading in the tree-shaded
pool? Perhaps we prefer a motto for each month, or

grandparents reading the Bible. If choosing the calendar looms so important, how much more vital it is to get the activities of this calendar linked to God by asking his blessing on each new day and year.

Dear God, help us to live each day of this year so well that our lives may seem now to be a part of thy Kingdom of Heaven.

JANUARY 2. *Even a child is known by his doings, whether his work be pure, and whether it be right.*— PROVERBS 20:11

On the first working morning of any new year, it is hard for the woman of the house to know where to "begin to commence to start." She stands in the center of the living room, and wonders what to touch first now that the children are in school and father is back at his job. If there is an older person or a baby at home, perhaps she wants to sit down with them and just think back over the bright moments of the holiday. This is a wonderful morning to get the heart organized for right action. If many different kinds of things can be enjoyed in this busy day, then the year may be filled with accomplishment.

Dear Father, help us face up to our need for spiritual organization and to keep our hearts right as we serve thee in our homes.

JANUARY 3. *Lift up your heads, O ye gates: and be ye lift up, ye everlasting doors; and the King of glory shall come in.*—PSALM 24:7

An old proverb says that a family's home is its castle, and it is just as true that the doors may open upon a temple. For when there is a knock at the door of any home, the neighbor or friend who stands there is a person made in the image of God. Making such visitors welcome is one of the joys of the household, often taken for granted. When an atmosphere of friendliness is projected in the home, then the spirit of God comes to prevail, and this loving warmth can be felt by family and visitors alike.

God, come into our hearts and homes even as the psalmist sang of thy entry into the beautiful temple.

JANUARY 4. *Be not forgetful to entertain strangers: for thereby some have entertained angels unawares.*—HEBREWS 13:2

It is so easy to put off entertaining friends, or allowing the children to bring their schoolmates home for a meal. "Next week we will not be so busy" is the hopeful remark in many a family but the next week brings its own demands. When simple entertainment of guests is pushed

11

to one side for too long this soon becomes a way of life. It takes real will power and social strength to right the picture and make fellowship a happy habit. This first week of the new year is a good time to make a beginning by inviting an old friend or new to share the family dinner.

God, for the joy of having friends in our homes, accept our thanks. Keep our hearts fit for friendship with thee.

JANUARY 5. *And ye shall seek me, and find me, when ye shall search for me with all your heart.*—JEREMIAH 29:13

When the heart is only halfway involved in a project, whether it is making a dress, cleaning a house, or planting a garden, the work is twice as hard. Everyone knows this and longs for the power of enthusiasm. No place is this more needed than in the cultivating of the spiritual virtues of patience, courage, and cheerfulness. Just wanting these with all the heart can help to bring them into the home, where they will undergird all the members of the family, regardless of age or problem.

Father, as all the pressures of the New Year begin to press in upon our homes, keep our hearts intent on finding thee.

JANUARY 6. *In your patience possess ye your souls.*
—LUKE 21:19

Is there anything more exasperating than looking for a familiar object in its accustomed place and finding it missing? This may be the school book of a child, while the bus or car is honking in the driveway. Perhaps it is the pin which mother wants to put on the lapel of her suit jacket. It is easy to fly all to pieces when such a trivial happening delays a crowded schedule. If patience is needed then, how much more is it demanded when there is a true crisis, of illness or emergency. Patience needs to be cultivated daily in little happenings, so that it sustains the soul through all of life's problems.

Lord, we do try to be patient, and we feel guilty when we fail. Please help us to grow more patient under tension.

JANUARY 7. *Sing unto the Lord, O ye saints of his, and give thanks at the remembrance of his holiness.*
—PSALM 30:4

Some days it is easier to sing than on other mornings, yet the birds manage to do it regardless of outer circumstances, such as weather. Looking out the window to try to trace the source of a bird song, one has a chance to turn from sighing to singing as one encounters the

13

rest of the world and moves away from solitary problems. A song is such a simple thing, and yet the memory of tunes hummed at the kitchen stove or over an ironing board makes a beautiful remembrance of a beloved mother. Why not try a song of thankfulness this very day?

Blessed Father, as we remember the songs of righteousness from the lips of beloved parents and teachers, we praise thee anew.

JANUARY 8. *And now abideth faith, hope, charity, these three; but the greatest of these is charity.*—I Co-RINTHIANS 13:13

Some verses of scripture are so well known that most of us take their truth for granted and don't even stop to consider what the words mean. Sometimes a word becomes out of date as new meanings come into the language. Old fashioned "charity" is such a word of virtue, and its revival and daily use can make for much happiness in the home. Reduced to its simplest terms it means consideration for others in a loving fashion, whether it involves spiritual attitudes or tangible aid. Each day offers opportunity to live in charity with our neighbors.

Loving Father, we are so grateful that thou art charitable to us and we want to learn to act with more charity toward others.

JANUARY 9. *The fear of the Lord is the instruction of wisdom; and before honour is humility.*—Proverbs 15:33

The best cook in any church or club didn't get that way in one making of the recipe. Probably her favorite cake or pie has been baked many many times for family and close friends before it is shared with a larger group. Meanwhile those who find cooking a hard chore stand aside thinking the good cook has some special secret. If she does have, it probably lies in trying humbly to make each cake a little better than the last, and practicing in many attempts to feed her family as best she can. Humility is almost always a prerequisite of honor, and it is something which anyone can learn in daily tasks.

God, as we serve thee in humble capacities in our homes, let these tasks be acceptable as reverent service to thee.

JANUARY 10. *For where your treasure is, there will your heart be also.*—Matthew 6:21

Each month there seems to be a day of reckoning with bills and budgets. Those who advise professionally on financial matters try first to find out what an individual or group really considers important enough to use as a goal for saving money. What are the true desires of

15

the heart, these counselors endeavor to find—whether education, travel, a new home, or a gift to some worthwhile cause. When a decision is reached, all the sacrifices seem easier. So it is when one has decided to share material resources as a steward of God.

God, often we are troubled by money matters. Please help us to know that eternal treasures are bought with coin of the heart.

JANUARY 11. *Comfort ye, comfort ye my people, saith your God.*—Isaiah 40:1

The arms outstretched to welcome the small child who has tumbled on the grass, the hand offered in a firm clasp to the one who has met with deep sorrow are gestures recognized in this modern day as means of comforting others. Sometimes it is hard to know what to say, but anyone can offer the silent touch of an understanding glance of sympathy. One of the oldest commands, coming from the Old Testament, is that of offering comfort; and the home is the place to start.

Father, we see the members of our families in need of comfort, and we bring their needs to thee in prayer seeking help.

16

JANUARY 12. *And we know that all things work together for good to them that love God, to them who are the called according to his purpose.*—ROMANS 8:28

Life is composed of so many parts—good, bad, and indifferent—that it seems hard to make them into one bundle which can be carried easily in the heart. Instead, the various parts shift as do the sticks of wood on one's shoulders when he is gathering wood for a campfire. Happy is the heart which has learned to accept all things into a busy life of service, using each new burden as a testimony.

Father, help us to assemble the various parts of life into one beautiful package which can be used by thee.

JANUARY 13. *He shall feed his flock like a shepherd: he shall gather the lambs with his arm, and carry them in his bosom, and shall gently lead those that are with young.*—ISAIAH 40:11

One of the most beautiful sights in the world is of a flock of sheep grazing on the green hillside, with the young snuggling close to their mothers. This is often a subject for photographs in books to read on a cold January day, or to study closely in a picture on the den wall. The gentleness of God in caring for his own is compared to the shepherd helping the young sheep to grow in strength.

Father, help us to walk close to thee just as the sheep recognize and follow their shepherd into green pastures.

JANUARY 14. *Fulfil ye my joy, that ye be like-minded, having the same love, being of one accord, of one mind.*—PHILIPPIANS 2:2

A way to lift the spirits from depression is to begin to think in terms of someone else—the neglected neighbor, the old friend who would appreciate a letter, the businessman who might enjoy a kind word when you shop for the tablet on which to write. For these people, too, have their moments of doubt and depression, even though it may look as though their lives are in much better shape than your own. Since we are made of the same hopes and ambitions, let us try to keep our "one mind" on cheerful, positive thoughts, thus helping one another to find more joy in daily living.

Father, accept our thanks for the happy times when we feel at one with life and those we love in thy beautiful world.

JANUARY 15. *Ye are my friends, if ye do whatsoever I command you.*—JOHN 15:14

There are many kinds of friendship in this life, but the dearest friends seem to grow out of shared experiences in working for a common cause. This is why community cooperation on various civic boards or church councils is one way to encourage newcomers to get acquainted, or oldtimers to come to see their associates in fresh perspective. Such earthly friendships seem to grow best when there is divine leadership through an earnest seeking for guidance as to how best to serve.

God, for this precious gift of friendship with thee, hear our earnest thanks as we try daily to express friendship.

JANUARY 16. *In the beginning God created the heaven and the earth.*—GENESIS 1:1

Along about the middle of the first month of the year, sometimes a feeling of depression sets in as resolutions are broken and holiday fatigue settles down into the year's routine. Then it is refreshing to remember that this is a wonderful world, made by God for the enjoyment of his children. Sometimes this fact is crowded out by the pressures of getting and gaining, so that when new blessings come into the home there is no time just to relax and enjoy them. When faced with man-made burdens, try remembering the beginning and know that God is here.

Father, when we are tempted to be depressed by modern confusion, help us remember that this world was created by thee.

JANUARY 17. *The Lord is my shepherd; I shall not want.*—PSALM 23:1

So many needs descend upon us as the year progresses—there is illness of a child, an older relative takes a bad fall, or there is the common cold to fight. One of the cures for all difficult problems is to try to reduce the situation to its simplest terms. It is easier to do this when repeating some helpful affirmation, and surely one which comforts in sorrow and blesses in joy is the simple reminder that we are the sheep of the heavenly pasture. Count to ten and repeat this beautiful reassuring phrase several times during the day, and watch your problems disappear.

God, take care of us as a part of thy great flock in the eye of the heavenly shepherd.

JANUARY 18. *He giveth power to the faint; and to them that have no might he increaseth strength.*—ISAIAH 40:29

With today's emphasis on strength and speed, it is easy to forget the promises of God in behalf of those who are weak. Sometimes we have to be made weak in order to find new strength since our old techniques obviously do not work for the greater problems. It is no sin to be weak and faint and in need of help, but it is wrong not to acknowledge the need for help. Asking God for help is the first step in securing what you need.

Gracious God, grant new strength for each day, and keep us from weariness of spirit and heaviness of heart.

JANUARY 19. *Search me, O God, and know my heart: try me, and know my thoughts.*—PSALM 139:23

With the pudding spilled on the sink drainboard, it is easy to despair on any busy day. So it is a real help when the mother says to a child, "I know you didn't mean to drop the bowl," or when a little girl lets her mother know that she is sorry she spilled the gooey mess. When families understand that there was no intent to make a mistake, it is easier to forgive and to go for the mop to make the floor clean again. If our hearts are right, there is no need to be burdened by failure.

God, regardless of the outer evidence of failure, look into our hearts and see that we are trying to live for thee.

JANUARY 20. *God is a Spirit: and they that worship him must worship him in spirit and in truth.*—JOHN 4:24

In this materialistic age, there are those who say, "If I can't see it and feel it, I don't believe it exists." Part of the problem of living today is reconciling the belief that the things which we cannot see with our eyes can truly be seen with our hearts, and perhaps give the greatest vision. When we are supported by such vistas of truth from the inner eye, it becomes possible to make outer dreams come true, whether planning a party dress, designing a birdhouse, or making up a story to put a sleepy grandchild into happy slumber.

Dear God, help us to feel thee in our hearts when we cannot see thee, and thus to manifest thy love to others.

JANUARY 21. *The Lord recompense thy work, and a full reward be given thee of the Lord God of Israel, under whose wings thou art come to trust.*—RUTH 2:12

Turning the dial on the television is often a signal for the releasing of confusing news into our homes. Hearing of injustices, and the tearing down of buildings or projects into which much time and money has gone, one cannot help having a sense of frustration. Then is when a person needs to practice a greater sense of trust in the God, whose great heart and healing wings encompass the world. The promise is that he will recompense the works of those who trust his love.

God of our troubled moments, as well as our happy days, teach us to throw doubt aside and to trust thee more.

JANUARY 22. *Behold, we count them happy which endure.*—JAMES 5:11

Have you ever seen the look of happiness which crosses the face of a child who has seen a simple project through to the end? It may be something so elemental as piling blocks on top of each other without their tipping over, or it may involve a teen-ager's successful attempt to climb the highest nearby hill. There is real satisfaction in coming to a moment of happy completion, and endurance is one of the joyful emotions of life, as well as being of help in sorrow and crisis. Healthy confidence comes through endurance.

Father, when we are tired, give us a fresh spurt of spiritual energy that we may find the will to be happy and endure.

JANUARY 23. *Blessed is the man that endureth temptation.*—JAMES 1:12

Temptation is one of the words which has fallen into bad days in this modern age of permissive behavior. Too often the old-fashioned word temptation is confused with a new opportunity to learn about the seamy side of life. A fresh temptation comes always to consider "temptation" an old-fashioned, rigid word. A part of overcoming temptation today involves accepting the ridicule in acknowledging that there are such temptations which must be endured in gaining growth spiritually.

Father, we do not mean to do right just to receive a reward, but we are grateful for the blessings inherent in righteousness.

JANUARY 24. *Sufficient unto the day is the evil thereof.*—MATTHEW 6:34

Often the young want to have all the world laid out before them, with each year plainly marked with new joys and adventures. One of the marks of maturity is to be glad for each new day as it comes, and thinking of it as a miniature lifetime in itself. Then one can surmount the evil which comes on that particular day, secure in the knowledge that tomorrow will bring new opportunities. Joys can be cherished today as peculiar to this day, and so kept as very special memories.

God, help us to remember that even as the evil of the day should be forgotten, so should be the good as we start again.

JANUARY 25. *But they constrained him, saying, Abide with us: For it is toward evening, and the day is far spent*—LUKE 24:29

A sad commentary each year is the fact that so many projects which the family intends to start are never even begun. They may have the feeling that already the time is past for success. Yet it is never too late to make a small beginning on what may turn out to be an exciting new project. Do you want to learn how to make a mosaic table? Then begin today with a tiny picture, or at least pick up the materials when you come home from shopping. Even the day which is "far spent" can be savored and enjoyed.

Father, forgive us for letting the days and the years go by without accomplishing our dreams before the time is far spent.

JANUARY 26. *Be ye angry, and sin not: let not the sun go down upon your wrath.*—EPHESIANS 4:26

The first month of the new year usually produces some rare and beautiful sunsets, vivid in their reds, violets, oranges, and greens. Since they are such a daily occurrence sunsets sometimes lose their meaning for those who watch, until some emergency like an accident or illness makes them aware of the blessing of each day. Then the sunset becomes the time to shake off the regrets of the day and the month, letting them dissolve with the brilliant colors into nothingness, leaving the heart free to start a fresh day in peace.

Father, it is so hard to keep from anger, and we are grateful for the advice to not harbor resentment beyond the sunset.

JANUARY 27. *But as for you, ye thought evil against me; but God meant it unto good.*—GENESIS 50:20

Often it takes years to see the true meaning and blessing in certain circumstances. If the early part of the year has its problems, perhaps these same situations will appear as blessings, even by the end of the current year. One way to make this happen is to try through prayer to search for the intent of God in the happening. Surely he does not mean for any of his children to be bitter through the hurt of any disappointment or sorrow. Turn the heartache over to him for healing that good may result.

God, so many things which seemed wrong at the time come to look right, so help us anew to trust thy will for our lives.

JANUARY 28. *For thine is the kingdom, and the power, and the glory, for ever. Amen.*—MATTHEW 6:13

Some phrases are whole mouthfuls of praise, and should be said slowly and repeated until their meaning falls into the subconscious mind. Such a phrase is the beautiful ending of the Lord's Prayer, which can serve to set at rest any feelings of insecurity in this world. The heart, which knows that true power belongs to God, has an inner resource to surmount the temporary power of illness, defeat, despair uncertainty, and the longing of unfulfilled desires. Each of us has the right and privilege of joining this eternal kingdom.

God, it is so good to know that the kingdom does belong to thee and that we may have a part in it through thy grace.

JANUARY 29. *Let the words of my mouth, and the meditation of my heart, be acceptable in thy sight, O Lord, my strength, and my redeemer.*—PSALM 19:14

A motto can be a real help in building a good life, day by day. Sometimes such mottoes need to change as the years go past, but it is also true that the experiences of life will bring new meanings to the same chosen motto. Nobody has to use the phrase which is helpful to a friend, but there is zest in finding your own special words of counsel and helpfulness, and then trying to put them into action in the daily routine.

Father, for the daily help from vital verses in thy holy word accept our thanks and make them truly part of our lives.

JANUARY 30. *My grace is sufficient for thee: for my strength is made perfect in weakness.*—II CORINTHIANS 12:9

No month is ever perfect, without its days of confusion. The trick is to make more good days than bad, and to balance out each day with good, even if the margin is very small. Thus do we grow in grace to meet the new tasks of the new month ahead. This calls for a slacking off of activities for a few minutes and sitting quietly and looking back on the joys and mistakes of the first month of the year. Can you see a tiny bit of progress? If not, then ask for strength to replace weakness, and the promise is that it will be granted.

God, when we are weary, hurt, or confused, give us the refreshing power of thy wonderful grace.

JANUARY 31. *And be ye of good courage, and bring of the fruit of the land.*—NUMBERS 13:20

Each one of us earns a different kind of spiritual fruit in the days of our months, for each task and set of circumstances is different. This makes for wonderful variety in living and what the psychologists term "flexibility." We can set our own goals by the thoughts of our hearts, and the flexing of our minds. The important thing is to take stock of the fruit which comes from the land of our daily living, and to be sure that we are producing and sharing as good citizens.

Father, forgive us the times we have failed to measure up to our resolutions, and help us with fresh courage each day.

February

FATHER, WE ARE AWARE OF THY
GREAT LOVE AS WE MARK THE HOLI-
DAYS OF PRECIOUS HERITAGE. GRANT
THAT WE MAY EXPRESS LOVE IN OUR
DAILY CONTACTS IN HOME, CHURCH,
AND COMMUNITY.

FEBRUARY 1. *And ye shall not swear by my name falsely, neither shalt thou profane the name of thy God: I am the Lord.*—LEVITICUS 19:12

At the beginning of any new month, it is important to be reminded with direct simplicity of the power available to help us meet the chores and problems ahead. Such a power is the simple phrase "I am the Lord," which serves as a reminder that trivial and petty problems can dissolve under his guidance. If his word is held in reverence this strength can be directed into everyday channels. The worst way to profane the name of God is not to try to do his will in home, school, business.

God, in this new month help us to keep thy name holy in our thoughts, words, and actions.

FEBRUARY 2. *I rejoice therefore that I have confidence in you.*—II CORINTHIANS 7:16

Sometimes surveys are taken to find out the words which are considered the most beautiful in various languages. In such inquiries familiar words such as "home," "love," "mother," "family" usually rate high. And there is a precious phrase which means much to everyone at any age in life—a child learning to ride a bicycle, a young woman accepting her first office job, or an adult moving into a new position. That is the happy sentence, "Of course you can do it." And we learn confidence by doing.

Father, we are glad that thou dost have confidence enough in us to trust us to learn how to solve problems and grow in grace.

FEBRUARY 3. *And he withdrew himself into the wilderness, and prayed.*—LUKE 5:16

Each of us needs his own special place of "wilderness," even if this has to be a tiny spot behind a door which opens into a bedroom or even the hallway. Admittedly it is hard to find a special place for aloneness in the busy, crowded age of apartments and small yards in subdivisions. Yet the importance of seeking out such a place cannot be overestimated, for we have the example of Jesus to whom it was important. For having a place of quiet makes it easier to pray, and prayer accomplishes much.

Father, help us to keep a special place in our hearts where we can withdraw and commune with thee and find new strength.

FEBRUARY 4. *The righteous also shall hold on his way, and he that hath clean hands shall be stronger and stronger.*—JOB 17:9

What a wonderful moment it is when a child learns to pick up an object and hold it in tiny hands or offer it to the hands of his parents. And it is an equally important day when a grandparent who has suffered injury or illness comes to the place where once more he can feed himself with sure fingers. Strength seems to come from using what strength is available. We can see this when using our hands, and it is as true within

32

the heart where growth cannot be seen so easily by others, but can be felt by the individual.

Dear God, give us persistence that we may practice the difficult virtues and thus grow from strength to strength.

FEBRUARY 5. *Little children, let no man deceive you: he that doeth righteousness is righteous, even as he is righteous.*—I JOHN 3:7

When the little boy asked his grandfather what was being planted in the good earth, the wise gardener answered that the seed knew exactly what it would become when the sun and the rain and time had a chance to help it grow. The little boy was delighted to learn that a carrot is always a carrot, and a carnation is always a carnation. So it is that righteousness comes from righteous action, and there is no deviation in the garden of life.

God, for the fellowship of those along the way who are trying to live in righteousness, accept our thanks this day.

FEBRUARY 6. *It is better to dwell in the wilderness, than with a contentious and an angry woman.*—PROV-ERBS 21:19

A young woman envied a beautiful home near her own, and driving by on her way to work she would imagine how perfectly appointed the house was inside. When she came to ring the doorbell on a drive for community funds, she was surprised at the sound of loud voices in the living room. Waiting for the door to be opened, she heard the end of a quarrel involving money, and was not surprised when her request was denied. Next morning as she drove past the house, she had a different concept of its beauty, for she knew of the contention between people which spoiled the appearance.

Lord, keep us from being angry at petty things and thus making life difficult for those dear ones nearest us.

FEBRUARY 7. *The Lord shall open unto thee his good treasure, the heaven to give the rain unto thy land in his season.*—DEUTERONOMY 28:12

People often seem to be divided into two kinds—those who enjoy a rainy day, and those who find the rain depressing. Yet in the early months of the year almost all parts of our nation can expect showers, even as the pattern may be reversed in other nations in different time zones. Showers fall in all parts of God's world as a part of his pattern for growth. Just so do the days of tears, or the moments of depression come to each heart, but the promise is that they are a part of the ultimate treasure of God.

Father, help us to live wisely whatever rain thou dost send into our hearts and lives.

FEBRUARY 8. *I am the true vine, and my Father is the husbandman.*—JOHN 15:1

When kept to the house for any length of time, because of winter colds, or illness of a child, one has a tendency to feel alone and lonely. Then it is sometimes necessary to remind ourselves that each of us is a part of the vineyard of life, even a portion of the living branch. No matter how isolated we may be through illness, accident, or routine which seems boring, we are entitled to have vitality and life flowing in our hearts through the promises of God.

Father, when tempted to be lonely, may we remember our privileges as fellow workers in the vineyard of life.

FEBRUARY 9. *But thou, O Lord, shalt endure for ever; and thy remembrance unto all generations.*—PSALM 102:12

Often on a dark day there is a remembrance of things past, and a time to look at a scrapbook or a photograph album of the old home, or school-day friends. We have a deep sense of nostalgia for that which is gone, realizing that the past can never be recovered or relived, except in the memories of our hearts. It is then that we need to be reminded of the essential sameness of God, available to us at all ages and in all generations. We need a fresh perspective of God's time pattern for our lives.

God, forgive us for our impatience when we fret at the quick passing of time, for we know our frailties.

FEBRUARY 10. *Therefore I will look unto the Lord; I will wait for the God of my salvation: My God will hear me.*—Micah 7:7

As the second month of the year wears on, many financial and business details crowd the home calendar as well as the office. When budget problems threaten to cause hard words between loved ones, or create tension and fear, there is real value in recalling precious words from the Bible. Learning to trust God in money matters may be one of the most important lessons anyone can learn, and certainly is a vital one to pass along to children. There is no limit to the assurance, "My God will hear me."

Eternal God, we are grateful that thou wilt listen to us in our moments of deep despair and high hopes. Hear us now.

FEBRUARY 11. *And I will establish my covenant with thee; and thou shalt know that I am the Lord.*—EZEKIEL 16:62

One cause of worry and unhappiness is just plain inability or unwillingness to keep the promises made in good faith. It is so easy to look ahead and say, "I'll do this by the middle of the month." Then the time looms within the week, and the calendar is already jammed full with other events. There is a real temptation to alibi one's way out of the commitment for service. Inner peace comes in finding a way to follow through on a promise made, and this can often be done by remembering that God will help.

God, help us to keep our promises to those we love and to our friends, that we may be more worthy of thy covenant of grace.

FEBRUARY 12. *Sing forth the honour of his name: make his praise glorious.*—PSALM 66:2

The Bible is full of words of praise for heroes, as if to give a blessing to the normal wish of the heart to honor those who achieve. As the time comes when our nation remembers a man who loved his country and all its citizens, there is fresh opportunity to thank those who serve in modern-day capacities. Have you taken time to

37

write that letter to the young man in military service from your church? Abraham Lincoln found time to write notes of condolence from his burdened desk and heart.

God, we would honor thee with our lives, even as we remember those who serve their nations with heroism and courage.

FEBRUARY 13. *And he arose, and rebuked the wind, and said unto the sea, Peace, be still.*—MARK 4:39

The tendency in life today is to hold tightly to the emotions so that we do not become unduly involved in sentiment. Yet sometimes the winds of memory blow into our hearts so that we find it hard to pursue an even course on the sea of life. This is apt to happen when holidays crowd the calendar, particularly if those we love are away from us temporarily, or have been lost in life. There is comfort in remembering that in these circumstances there is one who can bring peace to the heart, through the practice of stillness in prayer, seeking guidance.

Father, when the winds of doubt assail us, give us power to rebuke them until peace returns to our hearts and homes.

FEBRUARY 14. *Let love be without dissimulation. Abhor that which is evil; cleave to that which is good.* —ROMANS 12:9

On the happy day of St. Valentine, it is fun to remember those we love, regardless of age. A look at any card counter shows the amazing variety of Valentines to meet all situations and all types of friends and acquaintances. We have a tendency to forget that true love should not be broken up into many parts and "dissimulated." Instead, one vital living strand of love should permeate all of life's activities, as an expression of appreciation of God's love for each of his children.

Father of love, let our love be united on earth with thy eternal kingdom of love.

FEBRUARY 15. *For the Lord hath comforted his people, and will have mercy upon his afflicted.*—ISAIAH 49:13

Grandmothers of an earlier generation always had a pair of "comfort" slippers, which they slipped into the minute they could take off the shoes in which they had done their chores. By resting their feet they were able to pick up the many duties of the new day. There is no shame in any generation in trying to make the body as comfortable as it can be as it serves us in our efforts to serve others.

God, show us how to put our love in action through simple acts which comfort those nearest us in joy and sorrow.

FEBRUARY 16. *Bless the Lord, O my soul, and forget not all his benefits.*—PSALM 103:2

How often when facing some difficult situation we say to ourselves, "I'll never forget how lucky I was to get out of this; if the way will just open for me to get away." Yet when the temptation or burden is removed, we are so overjoyed that we often fail to say a word of thanks to the one who provided counsel or funds, or who merely listened to our problem. Therefore it is easy to forget the goodness of God himself. One way to thank him is to be grateful to helpful friends.

Father, we neglect to thank our friends for kindnesses even as we forget thy goodness. Please forgive us both sins.

FEBRUARY 17. *Be thou prepared, and prepare for thyself, thou, and all thy company that are assembled unto thee.*—EZEKIEL 38:7

A wise teacher once said, "Remember that you cannot give to anyone else what you do not have yourself."

This obvious truth is often overlooked in spiritual matters. Yet no one of us would try to borrow a cup of sugar without taking an empty cup to be filled. We must offer our empty lives to God to be filled with blessings, and we must above all else be ready and willing to receive the good which is around us. Today is a good time to prepare for future happiness by expecting it to come into life.

God, we prepare our hearts now for thy blessings, asking thee to fill our lives that we may be able to share with others.

FEBRUARY 18. *And be not faithless, but believing.* —JOHN 20:27

A friend who had recently been left alone in her large house said, "I would get along all right at night, if it were not for the scare stories of my friends." Instead of counselling her to have faith that all would go well with her and that she could learn the art of living alone, these individuals repeated stories of horror from television, radio, and newspaper. Thus they compounded the problem, probably without meaning to make my friend miserable. Faith is always a better choice than fear.

Father, when faced with the two sides of the coin of life, where we have a choice of doubt or believing, give us faith.

FEBRUARY 19. *But many that are first shall be last;
and the last shall be first.*—MATTHEW 19:30

It is disconcerting, to say the least, to stand before a door
in line with others, and then to have the manager of the
department store open another door first. Thus many
who have arrived early and expected to be admitted at
once, find themselves pushing at the end of a second
line. This is a simple illustration of what may happen
to the heart which smugly thinks itself safe and secure,
but which has an unexpected problem to face. The best
line of all is the path of service led by God.

Dear heavenly father, help us to know our proper place
in the kingdom of heaven, as loving servants of thine.

FEBRUARY 20. *How amiable are thy tabernacles, O
Lord of hosts!*—PSALM 84:11

Every housewife has the happy experience of encoun-
tering a routine day when for no special reason her heart
seems lighter than usual, and everything turns out a
little better than expected. Even the meringue on top
the lemon pie comes out the proper shade of brown,
and none of the cookie dough spills over onto the oven
but stays crisply on the pan. Then it is that home seems
a wonderful "tabernacle" of love and peace. Such
moments should be savored and enjoyed to the utmost
as special gifts of joy.

God, it is good to have a happy day and to feel at home in thy universe. Help us to keep our part of it beautiful.

FEBRUARY 21. *In the day of my trouble I will call upon thee: for thou wilt answer me.*—PSALM 86:7

It is the suddenness of change in the family routine which often presents the biggest problems to the homemaker. Just when it seems that everything is going smoothly, a child has an accident in the yard, or a tire goes flat during a trip to the super market, or a telephone call tells of an emergency of a friend. When trouble comes swiftly, it is good to be prepared in the heart. Immediately prayer can be offered with the expectation of an answer as to what to do next.

God of strength, we are so grateful that we do know where we can turn in time of trouble and truly find help.

FEBRUARY 22. *But glory, honour, and peace to every man that worketh good.*—ROMANS 2:10

As the time comes to celebrate the birthday of George Washington, first president of our nation, it is good to remember that the founding fathers hoped that each individual would contribute his best talents to the common good of all. This ideal is in line with the wonderful Bible assurance that to be good and to do good is the one sure way to peace followed by glory and honor. This high motive can sustain and bless us today in our hope for peace at home and in the world.

Father, we thank thee for the rule that working for good is the way to true honor, glory, and peace.

FEBRUARY 23. *For he is our God; and we are the people of his pasture, and the sheep of his hand.*—PSALM 95:7

In the modern world of the machine, it is easy to feel far removed from the pastoral life of the Old Testament, even if we still live on farms or in homes with trees and gardens. Somehow the feeling that we are the sheep of God's eternal pasture must be transferred into our hearts and carried with us, even if we fly in huge ships through the skies or plough across the seas. The soul's relationship of shepherd and sheep is still available to us.

God, help us to realize fully the joys and blessings of living as sheep in the protected pastures of eternity.

FEBRUARY 24. *In my Father's house are many mansions: if it were not so, I would have told you.*—JOHN 14:2

Scarcely a month of life goes by without its intimate personal sorrow in the loss of one who has been held most dear in the circle of friendship, or the falling of a national figure through accidental death or illness. When such times come it is a help to be able to remember the Bible's promise of heavenly mansions, a belief not generally shared in this modern day. There is real comfort in the inner assurance that each block of loving endeavor in this life can be added to the soul's home.

God of assurance, we rely on these blessed words of promise, knowing that there is truly a place prepared for each of us.

FEBRUARY 25. *And be ye kind one to another, tenderhearted, forgiving one another, even as God for Christ's sake hath forgiven you.*—EPHESIANS 4:32

Isn't it a real surprise to learn quite by accident that someone whom we had supposed led almost a charmed life of happiness has an inner problem we had never suspected? Learning this should make us more compassionate about the other people we meet in life, yet we seem to be more and more inclined to think the other person's life is easier than our own. A good policy is: When in doubt, be extra kind.

Forgive us, father, for judging others as we would not like to have thee judge us. Help us to express kindness daily.

FEBRUARY 26.   *For they that say such things declare plainly that they seek a country.*—Hebrews 11:14

In an era of diplomatic double-talk, when even routine forms to sign have ambiguous phrases which confuse many people, it is refreshing to find plain talk. This is available in the Bible, which declares firmly and proudly that there is a country which lies ahead for the spiritual pilgrim. How wonderful it is to know that there is a goal for the pilgrimage of life available to all who seek earnestly and in love.

God of the universe, who holds the map of the world confidently, help us make our way to the eternal city of light.

FEBRUARY 27.   *Enter into his gates with thanksgiving, and into his courts with praise.*—Psalm 100:4

In the window of the service porch of their new home, a couple placed a little pair of ceramic birds, which they would see as they put the automobile into the nearby garage. The large turkey had a spreading tail of brown feathers and an imposing red head and breast, while the turkey hen was in muted pastel colors. The two figurines faced each other in the window, reminding them that this new home was "the house of thanksgiving." Each day is meant to be a day of praise.

With joy we greet thee, Father, in our homes, churches, and daily activities. Keep us aware of thee and of one another.

FEBRUARY 28. *Ye shall not make with me gods of silver, neither shall ye make unto you gods of gold.* —Exodus 20:23

Sometimes it seems as if each month is more of a race to find the money to buy the necessary items for home, school clothes for the children, and funds for growing tax programs. In this rush and commotion it is easy to adopt unconsciously an attitude that the one thing in life which is important is the making and holding of money. Gold and silver are not meant to be treated as gods, but as useful approaches to the God of understanding and service.

God, may the commandments engraved on stone be inscribed with love in our hearts and translated into daily action.

FEBRUARY 29. *For he that will love life, and see good days, let him refrain his tongue from evil, and his lips that they speak no guile.*—I PETER 3:10

When the special day of Leap Year comes into the calendar, it brings birthdays to those who may not have been able to celebrate for the past three years. Such a special day deserves to be treated a little differently than the ordinary routine day, and one fine woman uses it for "extra things." She fills it with things she has wanted to do, but has not had time for, such as writing notes to old friends, trying a new recipe, making a call on a neighbor. She invests her extra day, and it pays dividends through all the days of the year.

God, in this extra day of life in our earthly calendar, help us to show our love of life through kind acts and gentle words.

March

LORD, FOR THE BLESSINGS AHEAD,
WE ARE GRATEFUL. WHATEVER THE
CLOUDY OR WINDY DAYS BRING, HELP
US TO BE MINDFUL OF THE COMING
OF SPRINGTIME WITH FRESH OPPOR-
TUNITIES FOR SERVICE.

MARCH 1. *And God made a wind to pass over the earth, and the waters assuaged.*—GENESIS 8:1

Two words which go together instantly and for always are "March" and "wind." Children welcome the month and breezes as a time to fly kites high in the sky, but adults sometimes dread this combination as a bringer of headaches or dust. Sometimes an element of fear centers about winds which can bring destruction. Yet in the beginning the wind was made by God to help the waters abate in making a beautiful world. So the winds of emotional storms sometimes are helpful in bringing a more stable world to the heart.

God, be with us when the winds of life threaten us, and help us to know that thou art in the storm as in the calm.

MARCH 2. *My glory was fresh in me, and my bow was renewed in my hand.*—JOB 29:20

As the grandfather walked back to the house he said, "I love a fresh day." To a child this word probably means a certain briskness which makes a red sweater feel good when he goes out to play. It may be a long time before he is old enough to know that the word "fresh" carries with it a feeling of newness and of better days with spring following winter. Happy is the heart which finds a daily freshness through prayer and asking divine guidance in old tasks.

Father, may our glory always be fresh in us as we face each day with new courage and hope based in thee and thy goodness.

MARCH 3. *The plowers plowed upon my back: they made long their furrows.*—PSALM 129:3

At the first sign of spring, the planting begins in all parts of the world. Sometimes it is done still with just a forked stick carried in the hand of a weary worker. Even when the ploughing is done with extravagant machinery there is much work involved in cutting furrows. It may be that the worker feels that his own back has been ploughed at the end of a day in the field. Often our hearts feel that way after a protracted illness in the family, but God can heal and bless.

God, take away the feeling of heaviness from our hearts, and give us fresh energy for ploughing our own fields.

MARCH 4. *Better is a dinner of herbs where love is, than a stalled ox and hatred therewith.*—PROVERBS 15:17

Kept indoors by rain or wind, one may choose between being bored by the weather, or making interesting dinner preparations. A bitter March day is a good time to cook a stew, with the aromatic perfume of herbs coming through the kitchen into the living room. What a good welcome home this fragrance is to the man of the house, who has fought the rain on the freeway, or tramped a country road. Such a simple meal with the family can be an integral part of the most beautiful memories of life.

Loving father, help us to make the most of each opportunity for fellowship within the family circle, blessed by thee.

MARCH 5. *Then Peter opened his mouth, and said, Of a truth I perceive that God is no respecter of persons.* —ACTS 10:34

It is easy to become resentful of one's individual fate and to feel that the other person has an easier life. This attitude becomes worse if financial circumstances are pressing, or aches and pains multiply with changeable weather. It takes a forthright person like Peter to point out what should be obvious to all of us—that God is no respecter of persons, but each of us has his own trials and tribulations. Fortunately the same God stands equally ready to help each who asks of him.

God, we ask thee now to give us hearts which see clearly the needs and desires of those close to us, and ourselves.

MARCH 6. *And my people shall dwell in a peaceable habitation, and in sure dwellings, and in quiet resting places.* —ISAIAH 32:18

From Old Testament times it has been the announced intention of God that his people should have their places

of rest. It falls to the homemaker to see that the dear ones
in the family circle have those resting places. For a baby
it is a crib, covered perhaps with a hand embroidered
quilt made by a loving relative. A growing teenager needs
his own room in which to think, even though this be
with the help of a record player or other noisemaker.
We never grow beyond the need of rest through meditation.

Father, forgive us our feverish activity, and grant us fresh
wisdom in discovering for ourselves the true rest in thee.

MARCH 7. *Who hath gathered the wind in his fists?*
—PROVERBS 30:4

A little girl once confided to her mother that she thought
the wind was a giant standing at the top of the world
who blew his breath over the seas and the land. She
wondered fearfully how to get the wind stopped once it
had such a good start. Many of us feel that way as we
see the winds of hate blowing across the world through
war, and we are one with the ancients who asked a similar
question. It is good to know that it is the hand of God
which controls the winds of eternity.

God, help us to trust our hands into thine, knowing that
thou dost have the winds of the world in ultimate control.

MARCH 8. *The trees went forth on a time to annoint a king over them.*—JUDGES 9:8

A gray day in early spring is a wonderful time to read stories and dream dreams. Some of the most interesting and imaginative tales can be found in the Old Testament. This passage which describes the attitudes of trees, symbolic of other desires of men, is one which should not be denied to a child. Even a few minutes spent with the Bible can bear much good fruit in later years when an adult remembers a happy afternoon of fellowship with the Book and opens it again, searching for helpful truth.

Dear God, we do thank thee for all the joyful experiences available to us through reading, expecially in thy word.

MARCH 9. *Lay up for yourselves treasures in heaven, where neither moth nor rust doth corrupt, and where thieves do not break through nor steal.*—MATTHEW 6:20

One of the most interesting treasure chests most of us ever encounter is the old trunk or box filled with cast-off clothing of older people. As children we love to dress up and pretend to be someone else, and as adults we like to look back to the past to see what were our own treasures when young. The doll brings back precious memories of the mother who made for it a muff and a hat out of a piece of fur. Treasures take many forms, and the most lasting are those which enrich our hearts.

54

Father, truly we want our treasures to be of thee, and to learn to discriminate between the good and evil, the better and best.

MARCH 10. *Forgetting those things which are behind* . . . —PHILIPPIANS 3:13

It is so easy to be nostalgic about the past. We can feel the very emotions we knew when living in a favorite house, even as we drive past it when visiting the former hometown. Sometimes it is so hard to give up the happiness of the past that we overlook the opportunities of the present, and are unable to plan tangible joys for the future. The church membership left back home keeps the newcomer from taking an active part in her new home. Forgetting the past is hard discipline, but a necessary prerequisite to new blessings.

Father, help me to forget wrongs and slights, but to remember kindnesses and try to duplicate them today.

MARCH 11. *Saul and Jonathan were lovely and pleasant in their lives.*—II SAMUEL 1:23

How wonderful it is to have a friend who makes life "lovely and pleasant." Sometimes such friendships survive the changing years and great distances, as new circumstances bring challenges which send friends into different countries. Yet there is a unity of heart and spirit which joins those who have shared loveliness. Today might be a good day to write that long owed letter to one who shared happy days and brought into life the loveliness which lasts and grows.

Father, we are grateful also for our friendship with thee, and ask that this may be evident in our other friendships.

MARCH 12. *So then because thou art lukewarm, and neither cold nor hot, I will spue thee out of my mouth.* —REVELATION 3:16

An invalid said to her pastor, "It is the days which change from hot to cold, and are just in between, which are so hard on my bones and constitution." Most of us know what she meant, for we can adjust to great heat by dressing appropriately, and we can always add another sweater on a rough, raw day. There is something innate in our natures about wanting things to be as they seem to be—one thing or the other. Perhaps this is a good ideal to follow in determining to count for righteousness.

God, we are sorry that so often we are lukewarm to good causes when we should lend our influence more forcefully. Forgive us.

MARCH 13. *Sing aloud unto God our strength: make a joyful noise unto the God of Jacob.* —PSALM 81:1

It used to be the custom in American life for families to sing together around the piano, and it has remained for television to bring some of this being together back into the home. How often do family trios sing country music, or groups of young people band into choruses which thrill listening audiences! Learning to sing together the great hymns of faith is one way to insure a subconscious source of courage when away from home, perhaps in military service. Is there a hymn in your heart now?

Father, in our tasks, we would sing gratefully, trusting thee to hear the words which often our hearts cannot utter.

MARCH 14. *Now these are thy servants and thy people, whom thou hast redeemed by thy great power, and by thy strong hand.*—NEHEMIAH 1:10

When the middle-of-the-month blues plague a household, it is well to remember just who are the members of the family. Each one is more than mother, father, child, because all are individuals made in the image of God and redeemed by his great power. None of us knows our full potential for good, and few of us try to reach it because of negative images which hold us back. Take a good look in the mirror sometime today, and thank God that you are permitted to be you.

God, keep us knowing always that we are indeed thy children and thus have the privilege and responsibility of true growth.

MARCH 15. *O Timothy, keep that which is committed to thy trust.*—I TIMOTHY 6:20

Many plays have been built around the sad fact that much of life is spent in picking up that which we have thrown away in haste or in anger. How wonderful it is to be able to hold onto that which is good, knowing its value while we have it in our possession. Only then are we able to share its goodness with others. The Bible admonition is to a young man, but the advice is good for all ages. Holding to it can keep one youthful.

God, help us keep our early dreams intact by striving to make them come true in our homes and reaching out toward others.

MARCH 16. *Now therefore fear the Lord, and serve him in sincerity and in truth.*—JOSHUA 24:14

Of a certain political figure it was said in his hometown, "We always know just exactly where he stands on the issues." Sometimes these were unpopular, making him the target for much abuse, but there was never any doubt as to his sincerity. Over the years this made for general wholesome respect for his qualities. Sincerity is a sustaining virtue which can undergird all of life, and anyone can learn it.

Father, without the sincerity of thy promises to us, life would be uncertain. Help us to grow in sincerity and truth.

MARCH 17. *He maketh me to lie down in green pastures.*—PSALM 23:2

There is something about the color green which is always refreshing to the eye and the heart. On this day noted for "the wearing of the green" and the joyous "luck of the Irish" there is opportunity to think of the beauteous nature of green in the early springtime. The shade implies the newness of growing things, which can lead to bountiful harvest. It therefore becomes important that the right seeds are planted.

Father on this happy day, we would plant the seeds of kindness and compassion that the harvest may be rewarding with joy.

MARCH 18. *The Lord is my portion, saith my soul; therefore will I hope in him.*—LAMENTATIONS 3:24

Dividing the food into proper portions at the family dinner table is a daily occurrence. Sometimes it is father who presides, or mother, or perhaps the dish is passed for the children to help themselves, not forgetting the tiniest, whose plate is in charge of an older brother or sister. Each of them needs other food—that of the heart, which gives the assurance that the Lord is the true portion, giving daily blessings.

Father, help us to know from whom our food and clothing come, since thou art the creator of the universe and giver of good gifts.

MARCH 19. *But make me thereof a little cake first, and bring it unto me, and after make for thee and for thy son.*—I KINGS 17:13

What a privilege came to this woman of scripture, since she was invited to make a little cake for the Old Testament man of God and to serve her son and herself from the same substance. There is power and joy today in realizing that the same system works in modern kitchens when baking good things for our loved ones. The first portion goes to God when our hearts are dedicated to serving him through the loving tasks of our hands.

God, keep our hearts and hands in perfect balance with thee, as we extend the borders of our homes to include others.

MARCH 20. *I shall go softly all my years in the bitterness of my soul.*—ISAIAH 38:15

Everybody knows someone who seems to have taken this tragic verse as a motto for living. All of us do it occasionally, particularly when days are dark and gloomy physically or emotionally. Bitterness accomplishes nothing positive, but is a negative force shriveling the soul and sending chills across the heart. Even as the sun comes out on a dreary day it is possible to let bitterness be warmed out of the heart through loving thoughts of forgiveness.

Father, when it is hard to forgive, grant us the extra strength which makes it possible, so we may walk in the sunshine.

MARCH 21. *O Lord God, turn not away the face of thine annointed: remember the mercies of David thy servant.*—II CHRONICLES 6:42

What a help it is when somebody speaks for us the words we feel in our hearts but are unable to phrase properly. David did this for so many through the Psalms. All of us feel we are servants in life, trying to do the tasks the days and months and years place before us, and we long to have God remember that we are in need of him. Today he will turn his face toward you in kindness if you ask.

Loving God, do not let us feel thee so far away from our earthly problems, but come into our hearts more fully and stay with us.

MARCH 22. *For if a man think himself to be something, when he is nothing, he deceiveth himself.*—GALATIANS 6:3

The proof of this verse is easily visible in modern life when phonies are encountered in business or social groups. Yet new discoveries in the field of science and psychology are proving that the opposite also is true—we deceive ourselves when we think we are less than we have the power of becoming. In order to succeed, it is necessary to hold to the positive image of good in the face of negative circumstances.

Father, we would become the most and the best that our talents permit, and we thank thee for this opportunity to grow.

MARCH 23. *My days are swifter than a weaver's shuttle, and are spent without hope.*—JOB 7:6

This double-jointed verse has two emotions packed into one sentence. Sometimes conflicting feelings are a part of the average day. Most of us find the days too swift to accomplish all that we dream about, but this is no reason to be without hope. Instead, the swift weaving of the shuttle should help us make our dreams come true, as we set up a pattern including family, friends, our church, and country.

Father, in the swift passage of the days, it is good to have thy companionship. Help us to use time wisely for thee.

MARCH 24. *Blessed is he whose transgression is forgiven, whose sin is covered.*—PSALM 32:1

A most unpopular word today is that tiny one, "sin." Many permissive schools of thought would take it out of the vocabulary entirely. Doing this would remove also one of the best feelings in life, that of receiving forgiveness for wrongdoing, or a renewal of a friendship after the overlooking of a fancied slight. If sin or regret plagues you this springtime, there is always a chance to change the pattern and know the blessedness of a restored relationship.

Lord, show us how to live graciously with each other, secure in the knowledge that our sins are forgiven and forgotten.

MARCH 25. *The north wind driveth away rain: so doth an angry countenance a backbiting tongue.*— PROVERBS 25:23

Certain weather signs mark every calendar, and it is usually true that when the wind comes out of the north the rain disappears. Sometimes this is an advantage if an early picnic is planned, but it can be a disappointment if water is needed for the recently planted seed. It is just as true a sign in life when gossip from a backbiting tongue is discouraged by a face which is angry at such trifling small talk, belittling another. Gossip can spread like a gusty north wind if not stopped in time.

Father, as we grow in grace, let our tongues be more quick to praise than to condemn.

MARCH 26. *For truly my words shall not be false: he that is perfect in knowledge is with thee.*—JOB 36:4

Calling to her children who were wondering what to do indoors on a gray March day, the mother said, "Why don't you look inside the big book of pictures, and see if you can find something new that will be a true story?" Soon the children were eagerly engrossed in learning about dogs and kittens from the pictures and text. There is great joy at any age in learning new truths about this interesting, wonderful world.

Father, at a time when there is so much false knowledge and so many rumors, keep our hearts anchored in thy truth.

MARCH 27. *He sendeth the springs into the valleys, which run among the hills.*—PSALM 104:10

When rain falls on the parched land, it is good to remember that some of it is going deep into the earth to help replenish the springs. How they continue for so many never-ending years is wonderful proof of the goodness of God to his children. So it is when the rains come into the human heart through tears at the loss of loved ones; a part of the spiritual rainfall goes deep into the soul to help restore and comfort others when they encounter the barren places of life.

Father, as we climb the hills of life, let us remember the springs of mercy which run in the valleys of discouragement.

MARCH 28. *Let not your heart be troubled: ye believe in God, believe also in me.*—JOHN 14:1

All day long the little word "let" is being used over and over in many households. The daughter says, "Mother, let me have this new dress," or a father says, "Yes, son, I will let you have the car." There is almost frightening power in such a tiny word which grants permission for special action. Yet without our having to ask, each individual is urged to just "let" his heart turn from trouble to peace through belief in God and his son.

Father, we are grateful for the privileges of salvation. Let us remain true to thy teachings always.

MARCH 29. *Thou, O God, didst send a plentiful rain, whereby thou didst confirm thine inheritance, when it was weary.*—PSALM 68:9

Before this month ends it is good to have "a real good soaking," for it makes all the springtime better in the abundance of fragrant flowers. There is reassurance in the annual recurrence of the seasons, some of which must bring the rainfall needed for the land grown weary. So it is when the fields of our activities seem parched and dry and given to dullness that we need to ask for showers of God's spirit.

Father, we grow weary in well-doing, and we need the stimulation of showered blessings from thy Holy Spirit.

MARCH 30. *If ye be come peaceably unto me to help me, mine heart shall be knit unto you.*—I CHRONICLES 12:17

A woman who loves to knit sets for herself certain goals within the month. She likes to put the last stitches into a sweater as the final days of the month appear on the calendar, so she will have something new to wear in the season ahead, or a gift completed for a birthday. A knit stitch binds into the next so that there is warmth and comfort for the wearer. So it is with friends who try to help each other in peace as they knit strong bonds of love.

Father, may we always try to help and not hinder, and so know the great joy of being knit into fellowship with thee.

MARCH 31. *I will open rivers in high places, and fountains in the midst of the valleys.*—ISAIAH 41:18

When the rivers are full but staying within their banks, there is a feeling of satisfaction, for this makes possible many blessings in the future. Water will be available for crops and for swimming pools for happy, splashing children. As the month so often given over to rain and storms goes into the past, there is an excellent time to reflect on the blessings which have come into life through emotional storms. Is the fountain of joy clear and bubbling in your life now? It can be, as you move with faith into the month ahead.

God, accept our thanks for this month of life, leaving us now for eternity. Help us to grasp the opportunities for service.

April

GOD OF GLORY, WE SEE THEE MANI-
FEST IN OUR GARDENS AS BULBS ARE
RESURRECTED FROM EARTH TO BLOS-
SOM. MAY WE LEARN TO GROW IN
THE GRACE AND BEAUTY OF THY LOV-
ING SPIRIT.

APRIL 1. *The fool hath said in his heart, There is no God.*—PSALM 14:1

On the first day of April, many are the surprises in happy families. Perhaps sugar appears in the salt shaker at the breakfast table. This prompts many giggles and chuckles from the children. Such lighthearted pranks in honor of "April Fool" are in stark contrast to the one real mark of the fool. The Bible says we are so identi-fied when we say there is no God. We can reverse this belief by faith.

God, keep our hearts light with the happy foolishness of shared pleasures, undergirded by the sureness of faith.

APRIL 2. *And the grace of our Lord was exceeding abundant with faith and love which is in Christ Jesus.* —I TIMOTHY 1:14

A lovely day in April seems filled with grace and beauty, and it is easy to feel an abundance of God's good gifts in each heart. Glancing out the window at the sunlight sparkling against the pale green early leaves on the blossoming tree, the eye comprehends more than this visible loveliness. The view includes the vista of renewal, the assurance of the coming of spring, with its reminder of God's goodness in grace, faith, and love.

God of grace, grant us a renewal of faith and love, even as the return of April brings another springtime of beauty.

APRIL 3. *The flowers appear on the earth.*—SONG OF SOLOMON 2:12

When the little girl found the first daffodil blossom of gold at the top of its green stalk, she asked her mother where the flower had been until this moment. Wisely the parent answered that the flower had been in the earth, but this was the proper time for its appearing in the garden of the home. All of life's best gifts are here in the earth, waiting our claiming them at the right time in the right way.

Dear God, let the beauty of the flowers of spring be reflected daily in our happy hearts serving through sunshine and shower.

APRIL 4. *And over it the cherubims of glory shadowing the mercy seat . . .*—HEBREWS 9:5

An old gardener arriving for clean-up chores at a home in springtime said, "Ah, this is a day for the angels." Surely in spring the cherubs of glory seem to hover over the garden, even though they cannot be seen. The birds and the butterflies may act as their representatives, or so it would seem on a fragrant morning. Whether or not this flight of fancy is true, we have the promise that the cherubims of glory shadow the mercy seat of God. We may approach it whenever in need.

Father, let us know always that we have the privilege of accepting help from thee in whatever form it may appear.

APRIL 5. *And can I discern between good and evil?*—II SAMUEL 19:35

One of the difficult decisions in any garden is whether the small green shoots are flowers or weeds. The earlier the determination can be made, the easier it is to root out the weeds and give the flower plants the most room for growth. If this is true in the garden, how much more important is it for the heart to decide which are the attitudes to discard and which to encourage to grow.

God, today may we be given wisdom to discard negative impulses and make room for growth of positive thoughts.

APRIL 6. *With good will doing service, as to the Lord, and not to men* . . .—EPHESIANS 6:7

The attractions of nature are so appealing in spring that it is hard to concentrate on the duties and tasks of group service. "Let's run away today and forget our chores" may be the advice over the telephone, and sometimes such respite is needed. Spring also furnishes an opportunity to revive the spirit and resolve to undertake service with a right good will, serving with a happy heart.

Father, forgive us for not keeping our hearts as well ordered as thy bountiful world of orderly natural beauty.

APRIL 7. *For I have learned by experience that the Lord hath blessed me for thy sake.*—GENESIS 30:27

A spring day often brings back memories of past happiness. Perhaps a lovely day is remembered through tears, as an April rain softens the landscape. From such nostalgic moods can come a strengthening of resolve based on the knowledge of trusted experience. Even difficult situations can lead to fresh energy for new forms of happiness.

Father, we are grateful for the times when thou hast blessed us by experiences which make us useful to others.

APRIL 8. *The Lord God hath opened mine ear, and I was not rebellious, neither turned away back.*—ISAIAH 50:5

The sounds of springtime bring new melodies into the home. First there is the haunting call of a bird flying on its migration. Soon there may be many songs in the garden. In early morning hours or at the quiet calm following sunset, it may be possible even to hear the soft whir of their feathered wings. Listening to the sounds of nature can quiet the heart and soothe a rebel spirit.

Father, we do wish not to be rebellious, but to do thy will as we go forward. Keep us from turning back from duties.

APRIL 9. *And all the women that were wise-hearted did spin with their hands.*—EXODUS 35:25

Spring housecleaning sometimes calls for the opening of the linen closet, or a drawer fragrant with old lavender. The family intends to use sometime the handwoven linen scarf, but somehow forgets it during the year. Perhaps the lovely cloth serves its purpose if even occasionally it is admired, and the one who made it is remembered with love. Work with the hands has for generations been therapy for women, and there are many new patterns and designs available in the current age.

Father, help us to use wisely whatever agencies of relaxation are available for our hands and our hearts.

APRIL 10. *The Lord is my light and my salvation; whom shall I fear?*—PSALM 27:1

Light of the sun in April adds much joy to each new morning. As the sunlight seems a little brighter in appearance it gives a little more warmth in the middle of each day. We begin to see more clearly what needs to be accomplished in the home and the garden. Sometimes the light of spring shines into the dark places of our hearts where fears linger, and we need to let this light of God come to bless and heal.

Lord of light, illumine our daily living. May we see aright the pathway of Christian service.

APRIL 11. *For to be carnally minded is death; but to be spiritually minded is life and peace.*—ROMANS 8:6

Against the beautiful backdrop of nature in spring, the word which comes from news reports often seems shocking in the extreme, as it tells of cruelty expressed in mass and individual crime. This contrast points up the need to leave the carnal mind behind, and to live within the spiritual mind where there is life and peace. The only time we have to try to do this is now, regardless of present problems.

Father, help us put on the mind of the spirit. May we learn a little more each day about living in peace.

APRIL 12. *Come, and let us return unto the Lord: for he hath torn, and he will heal us.*—HOSEA 6:1

Often in April occur the special services of the church which deal with Easter, even though the date is movable and flexible according to the current calendar. Implicit in all such observances of whatever denomination or persuasion is the heart's inner wish to return to the Lord, secure in the knowledge of his eternal healing of earthly hurts and woes. If you are torn with grief, or indecision, or a petty problem, there is healing available this very day.

God, we forget that thou art always on the way to meet us when we remember to come again into thy presence as we do now.

APRIL 13. *But Peter continued knocking: and when they had opened the door, and saw him, they were astonished.*—ACTS 12:16

Smiling happily the neighbor said, "This springtime finally I have a good crop of roses." She said that she had met with failure in the early years of her garden until she learned how to cultivate the bushes. "I was determined to someday have a beautiful rose garden. Won't you come with me now and pick yourself a bouquet?" Here was a living example of the beauty which comes into existence when we continue knocking at the doorways of life.

Father, keep us from growing too easily discouraged. Let our persistence be answered as the door of faith opens wider.

APRIL 14. *Fear not, little flock; for it is your Father's good pleasure to give you the kingdom.*—LUKE 12:32

What is more pleasant to the sight than a group of sheep on the green hillside, with the little lambs frolicking near their mothers. In their friskiness there is a tangible reminder of the joyfulness of springtime, and the universal urge to kick up the heels in lively step. How fortunate that in both the Old and New Testaments, the writers used sheep and their flocks as examples to show God as the Shepherd whose help is available to each of us today.

God, grant us the sure knowledge that we are indeed each day the sheep of thy pasture, protected by thy love.

APRIL 15. *And be not conformed to this world: but be ye transformed by the renewing of your mind.—* ROMANS 12:2

What transformations take effect in spring! The brown hillside suddenly is covered over with green grass. The white sand of the desert becomes pink and lavender with delicate, fragile flower petals. The earth is renewed through the sprouting of the seed following the necessary rainfall. So it is important for us to keep on reading and putting into our minds new thoughts which can transform our minds when God grants us new strength for fresh tasks.

Father, we ask humbly that our minds may be renewed so that we may serve thee better with richer wisdom.

APRIL 16. *We wait for light, but behold obscurity;
for brightness, but we walk in darkness.*—Isaiah 59:9

Contrasts between light and dark moments or days are
particularly noticeable in the changeable month of April.
Sometimes we long for the sunshine, thinking dark
cloudy hours are here for too many days. Yet this is
April, and we know if we wait a little longer the soft
springtime light of sunshine will be here to bless. In all
the cloudy moments of life, it is important to keep on
waiting with good grace until the darkness leaves.

Father, forgive us the dark moments of depression, and
grant us patience as we wait for the sunshine of cheerfulness.

APRIL 17. *The fear of the wicked, it shall come upon
him: but the desire of the righteous shall be granted.*
—Proverbs 10:24

One of the marks of spring is that it produces desires in
the hearts of mankind. It may be a simple desire, like
planting a garden, or buying a new dress. Underlying
such wishes is the deeper desire for change in making
the yard a little brighter, or the wardrobe a little more
pleasant to the eye. Even so the deeper desires of the
heart for a better disposition, a less restless nature, can
be nurtured each new spring through hope.

God, grant us more of righteousness that our spirits may be undergirded to make whatever changes are needed in our routine.

APRIL 18.   *Knowing this, that the trying of your faith worketh patience.*—JAMES 1:3

A friend telephoned and said, "For no reason at all I've been so happy today." This was good news indeed, for she had just come through a trying period of life when the temptation was great to give in to whining and complaining and self pity. She had acted instead with silent courage and great patience, expressing the modern form of endurance which many of us find most difficult. Now she was blessed with inner happiness.

Father, may this be a springtime in which we see spiritual blossoms growing from the loving roots of patience.

APRIL 19.   *O Lord my God, I cried unto thee, and thou hast healed me.*—PSALM 30:2

An early sign of recovery from illness is when the patient asks to be moved closer to the window to see the sun, or is taken by chair out of doors. There seems to be healing in getting closer to what we call "nature" for want of a better term. The earth seems healed of its own hurts as the beautiful flowers of spring cover the barren spots. Healing of any hurt is available when the seeking heart turns to God.

Father, as the earth is fulfilled in beauty, give us a fresh assurance of divine healing for all human hurts.

APRIL 20. *And that ye study to be quiet, and to do your own business, and to work with your own hands, as we commanded you . . .*—I Thessalonians 4:11

A young couple who had just moved into a new home had visions of a beautiful yard. But the wife complained to an older friend, "I had no idea it took so much work to get the ground ready for grass, and that trees took so long to grow." This is one of the reasons we are commanded to work with our hands and keep busy at our own business. By tending our own yards the beauty of the community and the world around us is increased.

God, give us energy to do the work which thou dost intend for each of us to do in our own way, thus serving thee best.

APRIL 21. *The grass withereth, the flower fadeth: but the word of our God shall stand for ever.*—Isaiah 40:8

Cutting the fresh lush grass of springtime, and seeing how quickly the delicate pink sweet peas fade in their blue vase, one sometimes has a feeling of the impermanence of life in a swift rush of wonderment. We long to have the rose remain in the bud, and keep the white lilies from fading to golden brown. Even when earthly beauty fades, there is assurance of the never failing power of the word of God to bless and sustain.

Father, the contrasts of our little days and thy long eternity sometimes bewilder us. Let our faith grow in power and strength.

APRIL 22. *Nevertheless I must walk to-day, and to-morrow, and the day following . . .*—LUKE 13:33

Whenever the big word "nevertheless" preceeds a statement, there is the implication that there are obstacles to the fulfillment of the intention. Sometimes that seems to be true of the new dreams of the beautiful springtime. It becomes easy to abandon care of the garden because of insect pests, or to stop the craft class, or forget to entertain friends. Then is the time to determine to walk in the prescribed pathway one day at a time.

Father, walk with us, so that our daily paths of routine become filled with the joy of vision and service.

APRIL 23. *And this will we do, if God permit.*—
HEBREWS 6:3

Sometimes a brief verse carries a long message. These words echo across the centuries from the time of the earliest disciples into the lives of those who try to serve God today. It is important to plan the work of the committee or the church circle, but it is also good to recognize that there may be necessary changes due to circumstances and situations. In all things there is good counsel in adding, "If God permit."

God, we would do the things which are permitted to thy children, and learn to leave undone that which we should not approach.

APRIL 24. *Is there no balm in Gilead; is there no physician there?*—JEREMIAH 8:22

An old hymn turns this question around to give the testimony "There is a balm in Gilead." This is a tune which gardeners sometimes hum at work on their grassy slopes. For there is good medicine in working with the earth. And if it is not practical to get down on the knees in a good sized plot, there is always the possibility of a window box with herbs.

God of all growing things, we are grateful for the substances in food and medicine which help to heal when we need strength.

APRIL 25. *Wherefore lift up the hands which hang down, and the feeble knees.*—HEBREWS 12:12.

We get so used to seeing the outstretched hands of our friends offering fellowship and help that we tend to forget that the strongest of us sometimes have hands which hang down in discouragement. The tendency to take people and things for granted is one of the worst faults of busy people. Is there someone you should encourage this springtime?

Father, when we ourselves have feeble knees in walking the paths of service, strengthen us even as we remember others.

APRIL 26. *And they shall know that I am the Lord, and that I have not said in vain that I would do this evil unto them.*—EZEKIEL 6:10

Many in this modern age do not believe in evil or in punishment, but the many chores of spring seem to bear out this Bible verse. We know that God is the Lord through the way the laws of growth work—the seed brings forth after its kind, and the cultivating of the good plants calls for the culling out of the evil weeds and pests. This is a reminder to each of us to trust the true God.

God, we do try to honor thee, and we ask for thy forgiveness when we forget that there are righteous rules of living to follow.

APRIL 27. *Examine yourselves, whether ye be in the faith; prove your own selves.*—II Corinthians 13:5

A couple who had been married for many years continued to follow the plan of once each week going out to inspect their farm together. What had been done on foot with a few rows of beans finally had to be done in automobile over many acres, but they kept on examining what the workers accomplished under their orders. It was a happy tradition which resulted in progress. Such a plan works wonders in helping the heart grow in grace when time is taken to examine recent experiences involving faith.

Father, we are so prone to forget that we have a responsibility to examine ourselves. Help us to see aright and clearly.

APRIL 28. *For the wages of sin is death; but the gift of God is eternal life through Jesus Christ our Lord.*
—Romans 6:23

Paying for the watering of the new lawn seed may be simply a matter of handing some coins to the neighbor boy, but any transaction involves wages of one sort or another. In an age given over to labor and management committees on an organized basis, it is strange that many forget that sin has its own wages, which must be paid in full through psychological problems or hidden heartaches of loneliness. Yet eternal life is a loving gift.

God, help us to receive from thee, and to stop working for worldly wages which tempt and destroy.

APRIL 29. *For I perceive that thou art in the gall of bitterness, and in the bond of iniquity.*—ACTS 8:23

Compassion is one of the most blessed virtues of any age. This verse speaks of one who recognized the galling aspects of holding onto a bitter grudge. Springtime presents a fresh chance to throw aside all such bitterness and join in the renewal of life through rejuvenated attitudes of friendliness. Perhaps your compassion today will help restore a friendship.

Loving God, take away any dregs of bitterness, so that the cup of springtime may be filled with joyousness and hope.

APRIL 30. *Praise ye the Lord; for it is good to sing praises unto our God; for it is pleasant; and praise is comely.*—PSALM 147:1

When the comely month of April leaves the calendar behind for another year, there is opportunity to say "Thank you" to God for a beautiful month of shadows and sunshine. If they do not balance out in this particular year, they may be compensated for by another April in God's own good time. Surely the month has had its happy surprises as well as its testings. Thus spring in the heart and the world prepares for abundant blessings.

Father, each month of life is a precious gift from thee, and we are most grateful. Use us to thy honor.

May

GOD, IN THIS MONTH OF REMEM-
BRANCE, KEEP US EVER MINDFUL OF
THEE. LET OUR CONCERN FOR OTHERS
BE KEEN IN SORROW, AS WELL AS IN
DAYS OF HAPPINESS.

MAY 1. *These things have I spoken unto you, that my joy might remain in you, and that your joy might be full.*—JOHN 15:11

In many parts of the world, special festivals and fiestas involving flowers take place on this day. There is an essential joyousness in all such activities, whether they involve winding streamers around a maypole, or leaving little baskets of flowers and sweets at the doorways of friends and neighbors. It is a time for the fullness of joy, which is the heritage of those who love God, the giver of life and joy.

God, keep us from limiting ourselves to dreary activities, but help us to find new joys in greater service for thee.

MAY 2. *But the land, whither ye go to possess it, is a land of hills and valleys, and drinketh water of the rain of heaven.*—DEUTERONOMY 11:11

It used to be the custom in pioneer times for migrations westward to begin in the springtime. This first week in May seems a time for fresh beginnings, and most of them have both hills of success and valleys of striving. Always a wonderful promise is the rain of heaven, whereby showers of blessing fall on the land or into weary hearts.

God, refresh us for reaching out again toward our dearest dreams, as we ask for refreshing spiritual blessings.

MAY 3. *To him that overcometh will I give to eat of the hidden manna.*—REVELATION 2:17

A delight on a May morning is to go out into the fields and pick a fresh strawberry, or perhaps to find just a lush green slender twig or tall blade of grass. The very earth smells good, and it seems as though it must also be tasted through a fresh growing vegetable or fruit. This is another manifestation of the way God has provided manna for his children in natural ways as well as miraculous.

Father, for the hidden manna of the earth in the many blessings of daily food, give us thankful hearts.

MAY 4. *A sower went out to sow his seed: and as he sowed, some fell by the way side.*—LUKE 8:5

At the time of planting of seed, there is a tendency to try to put the tiny portions into even rows in the garden. But this is not always practical, for a vagrant wind will blow mischievous seeds to one side, and the hand often is not steady enough to follow the eye's design. That which falls by the wayside is often gathered by the birds, who repay with their songs of gladness. We need to sow generously and happily.

Father, let us be involved with the good seed of thy truth so that even that which falls by the wayside may be turned to a blessing.

MAY 5. *For every man shall bear his own burden.*—GALATIANS 6:5

When it comes time to plant a garden, each gardener must select his own seeds. Does he want asters or zinnias in the garden's alphabet border? It is his happy "burden" to decide, since he will have the joy of harvesting. Just so, a housewife has the task of cleaning out dresser drawers so she will be able to find her possessions more easily. Individual choices must be made in all departments of living, where each has his own burden.

Father, we are grateful that thou dost help us along the way, offering strength to help carry each special burden of life.

MAY 6. *And the word of the Lord came unto him, saying . . .* —I KINGS 17:2

This familiar phrase of introduction appears often, especially in the Old Testament. From time immemorial it has been within the province of God to try to get his children to stand still and listen. A fragrant day in May is made to order for such a purpose, for God speaks through the fresh pink rosebud, the scent of early lilac coming into the home at twilight. When we listen, it is possible to hear God's loving guidance.

Father, often we are lonely for word from thee, and we ask a special message of beauty to help us live better this springtime.

MAY 7. *A fugitive and a vagabond shalt thou be in the earth.*—GENESIS 4:12

The general term "spring fever" has been given to a certain restlessness which haunts a person when sunshine and showers of springtime point to distant places of long held dreams. Sometimes even a small jaunt to see an old friend will help to satisfy the longing for some nameless pleasure. Yet we are all essentially vagabonds on earth, seeking our heavenly homeland, of which spring is a happy messenger.

God, when we are restless, help us to find our rest in thee, turning our energies into constructive channels of service.

MAY 8. *The Lord is thy keeper: the Lord is thy shade upon thy right hand.*—PSALM 121:5

It used to be the custom to stitch a fresh sunbonnet each May to wear through the days of spring and summer. Today the approach is more likely to be a new suntan oil to prepare the skin for the bright rays of warm sunshine. Instinctively we long for shade when the brilliance overcomes us. In blinding circumstances of life, God is available as the shade, making sure that just the right amount of sun and shadow reach into the heart.

Father, protect us in sunshine and shadow, as we walk toward the light, meeting our problems and opportunities.

MAY 9. *Wherefore be ye not unwise, but understanding what the will of the Lord is.*—EPHESIANS 5:17

As the seasons return, sometimes there is a mood of remembering the things we wanted to do a season or so back and still have not accomplished. We procrastinate and are not wise in our use of time. Yet with each new season there is granted a fresh opportunity to renew dreams and set goals for success. Surely God wills the happiness of achievement for his children.

God, help us to start again and to hold fast our dreams with each recurring springtime of beauty.

MAY 10. *For my yoke is easy, and my burden is light.* —MATTHEW 11:30

A familiar sight in Old Testament countries today is a pair of oxen between a wooden yoke. Even though this is seldom seen in the modern age unless travel takes an individual to a country with ancient methods, the feeling of a yoke is well known. All of us feel we have around our necks the yoke of many distractions and activities. Into this busyness comes God's counsel and offer of help.

God, help us to learn to wear with grace the yoke of daily burdens, and to trust thee for a light heart and strength.

MAY 11. *As an earring of gold, and an ornament of fine gold, so is a wise reprover upon an obedient ear.* —PROVERBS 25:12

Nobody likes reproof, least of all when planning a spring outing or a new wardrobe. Yet sometimes a word of caution or constructive criticism, when accepted graciously, can add to a situation some touch of attractiveness which is as fine jewelry to a beautiful costume. If such an offer comes from a "wise reprover" in the family who loves us, it is good at least to listen with an obedient ear.

Father, we would improve our hearts this springtime, so please keep us from hurt feelings at times of criticism.

MAY 12. *Love worketh no ill to his neighbour: therefore love is the fulfilling of the law.* —ROMANS 13:10

A warm evening in May makes it a real delight to sit on the porch or patio, anticipating the joys of summertime. There is an air of neighborliness when families are able to be out of doors. It is easy to wave across the hedge to a neighbor, or motion toward a chair. Friendliness is one of the ways to express the neighborly love which is a part of the heritage of disciples of Jesus.

Father, for the opportunities of sharing our homes with neighbors and friends, accept our thanks.

MAY 13. *Thou wilt keep him in perfect peace, whose mind is stayed on thee: because he trusteth in thee.*
—ISAIAH 26:3

On a peaceful day in May when the birds sing and new flowers appear in the garden, it is easy to feel that peace is possible when the heart trusts in God. Even as the flowers and the creatures in the out of doors go their appointed ways of loveliness there is fresh inspiration to try to walk our own pathways with a peaceful, contented spirit. God promises this peace to those who trust his word and abide in his love.

God, we reach out after the eternal blessing of peace, and ask for fresh portions of it to use in our lives today.

MAY 14. *I watch, and am as a sparrow alone upon the house top.*—PSALM 102:7

Loneliness is one of the marks of the seeking heart. It implies the wish for something better than the present which may have its confining duties. Often in the midst of people we feel alone and seem to look at even those dear to us as from a distant point. In this we are one with

God's creatures of the natural world, for even the sparrow pauses on the housetop to gather new strength for certain flight.

Father, forgive us for giving way to a sense of loneliness when thou art so eager to help us soar above our burdens.

MAY 15. *Can thine heart endure, or can thine hands be strong, in the days that I shall deal with thee?* —EZEKIEL 22:14

Questions in the Bible have their modern application. As they are read the individual automatically wonders if his response to trial would be any better than that exercised in the far distant past. Modern developments in psychology tend to point to new solutions, but in the last analysis the facing of problems comes back to the summoning up of inner resources of courage. There is God's help for each testing in life.

Father, give us more courage than we have known before to face the greater tasks of the complex days and years.

MAY 16. *There remaineth therefore a rest to the people of God.*—HEBREWS 4:9

Whenever the word "therefore" is used in a Bible text or legal document, the reader knows that the word follows to a logical progression of thought and calls for a resolution of the situation. So it is a comfort to come upon the precious promise that there is rest inherent, in spite of the struggles and difficulties in trying to live right.

Father, give us inner rest as we meet the outer duties of daily work in our portion of thy wonderful world.

MAY 17. *He wakeneth morning by morning, he wakeneth mine ear to hear as the learned.*—ISAIAH 50:4

A friend to many who proves helpful in time of trouble and who enjoys the good times of life more than most explains her secret of vitality. She likes to waken early in the morning and think over her schedule. This is in keeping with good modern psychological thought, which believes we should focus our minds on accomplishment in a positive way. Waking early and listening for God's guidance can be effective.

God, truly we want to "hear as the learned," so that our actions may carry out thy purposes in our lives.

MAY 18. *Even so it is not the will of your Father which is in heaven, that one of these little ones should perish.*—MATTHEW 18:14

When the children of the family first encounter a baby bird which has fallen from its nest and cannot be nursed back to health, this is sometimes their first dealing with sadness. Even adults cringe at the thought of young animals suffering during freak springtime storms. Yet over the world there so often sweeps the agony of war with many refugees as well as the wounded and dead. Seeing a fallen bird in a home garden is a reminder to pray again for peace so we do not perish.

Father, help us to build our economic and social world along lines of peace where all may grow to fulfill thy will.

MAY 19. *And they made their lives bitter with hard bondage, in mortar and in brick, and in all manner of service in the field.*—Exodus 1:14

From earliest recorded history, certain men have had to serve others in bondage. This was particularly true when the olden fields were being prepared for harvest. Sometimes now, when slavery is prohibited, we make ourselves slaves of worry and critical habits, or become addicted to drugs in an effort to escape the slavery of routine. If "they" no longer can make us bitter, then we should not make ourselves into slaves for any unworthy purpose.

God, deliver us from the bitterness of any bondage to unpleasant memories or long held grudges of resentment.

MAY 20. *Lord, I believe; help thou mine unbelief.*
—MARK 9:24

The little girl came running to her mother to show her how far she had come on making the doll dress. When she asked for help in turning the hem, her mother said, "Dear, you can do it." At first the child shook her head— "no"—but then she picked up the dress and with chubby fingers began to press in the hem. As she did so, a happy smile spread over her face. She could do more than she thought she could, because her mother believed in her. All of us can offer the gift of confidence to others and accept it for ourselves.

Lord, take away the times when we cannot believe, and give us more days when we believe completely in thy great power.

MAY 21. *And wisdom and knowledge shall be the stability of thy times, and strength of salvation.*—ISAIAH 33:6

Stability is coveted by many, for life can be as changeable as a May breeze, sending the leaves of the trees back and forth as a rippling fan on the new lawn. In changing times it is good to know from the Bible that stability comes from two things—wisdom and knowledge. These are given for the asking to the child of God who petitions through prayer.

Father, we stand in need of wisdom from eternity, and knowledge for today, that our lives may be stable and filled with strength.

MAY 22. *That ye be not slothful, but followers of them who through faith and patience inherit the promises.*—HEBREWS 6:12

Spring housecleaning often brings to light valuable heirlooms which have been forgotten in the daily use of other dishes or linens. Such beautiful pieces recall the loving aunt who made the quilt, or the grandfather who carved the cherry wood bowl. In accordance with their promises made in life, the beautiful reminders now belong to others who also love them. And to those who work in the kingdom of God there are abiding promises as eternal rewards of faith and patience.

God, help us to hold fast to our heritage of truth and love in a generation which often scoffs and grows cynical.

MAY 23. *The wilderness and the solitary place shall be glad for them; and the desert shall rejoice, and blossom as the rose.*—ISAIAH 35:1

Often the desert comes into beautiful bloom in the month of May following wintertime rains. The usually neutral sand looks like a fallen rainbow, reflecting shades of pink, blue, and lavender, and having the legendary pot of gold under a mass of glorious golden blossoms. As the desert rejoices, there is a reminder that the heart's wilderness can come to beautiful perfection following emotional storms.

Dear God, help us to grow the gift of patience when faced with the barren places of life, that they may blossom in thy good time.

MAY 24. *Deck thyself now with majesty and excellency; and array thyself with glory and beauty.*—JOB 40:10

Writing from Paris in May a friend commented, "It is even lovelier than the books and the songs tell us, for every tree is like a ruffled pink or white parasol." She was saying that in the springtime even the earth arrays itself with "glory and beauty." Often we are too busy to stop to admire it. Every spring has its own special beauty to be remembered and used to help keep our hearts beautiful before God in service.

Father, we thank thee for lovely lives and for vistas of beauty encountered in our daily walks with thee.

MAY 25. *And blessed be his glorious name for ever; and let the whole earth be filled with his glory; Amen, and Amen.*—PSALM 72:19

Every beautiful day comes to the hour of sunset. When a well filled life arrives at its inevitable end, it should be the joy of the heart to bless the glorious name of God who gives natural blessings and the fellowship of human friends. Sometimes our vision is clouded by rain or tears, and it is then that we need to hold to the truth that the whole earth will be filled with his glory. To this promise the Psalmist added the double authority of a chorus of Amens.

God, in the sunset hours of the lives of our friends, give us comfort and the assurance of thy eternal glory.

MAY 26. *Verily, verily, I say unto thee, We speak that we do know, and testify that we have seen.* —JOHN 3:11

How wonderful it is when a friend says, "This is the way I make this spice cake your family likes so well," or "Have you tried this new way of pressing a hem in a dress?" There is validity in a personal testimony, whether it concerns the kitchen or a newfound spiritual truth. We miss the opportunities to say "My prayers were answered," or "Have you asked God to help you find more patience?" Anyone can learn the art of witnessing.

God, help us to know that a blessing becomes our own as we share it with others through helpful testimony to meet human needs.

MAY 27. *If it be possible, as much as lieth in you, live peaceably with all men.*—ROMANS 12:18

There is nothing more comforting in this life than a friend or loved one who understands that we have tried hard to succeed, and who still loves us when we fail to live up to our ideals. The Bible acknowledges that each of us has a personal struggle to face in learning to live at peace with all men. Our responsibility is to do the best we can daily with our innate personalities, striving to throw out hate.

Prince of peace, give us a stable inner peace, strong enough to withstand the frequent temptations to impatience.

MAY 28. *Settle it therefore in your hearts, not to meditate before what ye shall answer.*—LUKE 21:14

Modern psychology confirms much of the scriptural wisdom, particularly as it concerns that word "settle." The heart which has determined upon a certain course of action—even if that decision is not completely wise—

is well on the way toward accomplishment, as compared with the one who is bogged down with indecision. Just to "settle" a situation, and trust for its ultimate outcome for good, helps bring about that good outcome.

Father, we are glad that our hearts may be settled upon thee through thy Son Jesus, and we ask for an end to indecision.

MAY 29. *Then I saw that wisdom excelleth folly, as far as light excelleth darkness.*—ECCLESIASTES 2:13

A certain writing technique in short stories involves the moment of recognition when the chief character comes to realize what has happened to him. This moment of clarity and vision is important to everyone in his daily living, for it means that even from unhappy experiences of sinning and folly, he can come to see the joy of living in the light of trust and faith, walking in confidence with God.

Father, forgive us our sins, and help us to make greater strides toward realizing our positive goals of right action.

MAY 30. *And a book of remembrance was written before him for them that feared the Lord, and that thought upon his name.*—MALACHI 3:16

What began as a simple service of remembrance in behalf of the Civil War dead of America has extended across the world wherever American servicemen and women live out valiant lives of courage. Now many other countries pause to respect the sacrifices of the slain and to recall others of their honored dead. This day in May marks the time of placing flowers on graves, and fresh resolves for peace in the heart.

God, for our precious memories accept our thanks, even though they come back to us through tears. Grant us the sunlight of peace.

MAY 31.   *O taste and see that the Lord is good: blessed is the man that trusteth in him.*—PSALM 34:8

As the month of May fades into the calendar, as the flowers wilt on the graves of loved ones, there is no time for continuing sorrow and looking backward with nostalgia. Instead there may be renewed joy in remembered blessings on which to base a more friendly life in the future. Repeatedly comes the invitation to each person to trust in God and enjoy his blessings.

Father, we thank thee for the beautiful memories of May, and ask that they may be built into a happy future of service.

June

GOD OF OUR HAPPY HOURS, WE RE-
JOICE WITH SCHOOL GRADUATES AND
THOSE PLEDGING VOWS IN MARRIAGE.
MAY OUR HEARTS BE YOUTHFUL AS
WE FIND JOY IN NEW SITUATIONS
AND CHANGING CIRCUMSTANCES.

JUNE 1. *Thou wilt shew me the path of life: in thy presence is fulness of joy.*—PSALM 16:11

When the poets sing of the beauty of a rare June day they are expressing the feeling of abundance and joy which fills the lives of many as this month begins. Always there are memories of joyous wedding days, and the anticipation of sharing in the happiness of this year's bridal couples pledging their vows in the presence of friends and families. Such beautiful moments in June are blessed with fullness of joy when God is honored.

Heavenly Father, grant thy precious blessings on all our joyous moments in this month of beauty and loveliness.

JUNE 2. *And above all these things put on charity, which is the bond of perfectness.*—COLOSSIANS 3:14

Opening her eyes and running to the window in her bare feet the little girl said of the June morning, "It looks like perfect outside." Sometimes adults fail to share this feeling because they are so busy with the trivial tasks of getting breakfast or planning the day's schedule that they do not have time to look at the "perfect." This keeps them also from living in "charity" or loving compassion with their neighbors, but the Bible links such actions with perfection.

Father, when the June days are so perfect, may we be reminded to try again for charity and perfection in our daily lives.

JUNE 3. *Thy testimonies also are my delight and my counsellers.*—PSALM 119:24

One of the delightful features of any month is the celebration of the birthday of a family member or friend. Then is a good time to consider what are the special characteristics of that person which add to group happiness. Sometimes it will be a loving spirit, an understanding heart, or the ability to comfort when a friend is in deep distress. Such people often have special verses which are mottoes, and have found in God the guidance with which to counsel, expressing great delight in his law.

Father, for the birthdays of those who matter to us accept our thanks, and help us all to be born into thy kingdom.

JUNE 4. *Be ye therefore followers of God, as dear children.*—EPHESIANS 5:1

Sorrow sometimes comes in a beautiful month such as June. Then there is poignancy in the heartache contrasting with the delicate flower petals and the fragile markings of the butterflies over the green grass beneath the faithful guardian trees. Yet in all experiences, joyous and sad, we are admonished to be followers of God, accepting life as dear children of a loving father.

God, help us to use grief and loss as stepping-stones to fulfillment, and not hoard them as selfish sorrows.

JUNE 5. *And Elisha said unto him, As the Lord liveth, and as thy soul liveth, I will not leave thee.*—II KINGS 2:2

School-day friends find June a month of parting. Often there is heard the lament, "I don't want to leave you, but I have to." This is the way of life. At the base of many marriages is the overwhelming longing to belong to someone who will not leave. Yet all are lonely until we find our rest in God. Undergirded by his love, we see that partings and beginnings are made easier. When God remains with the person, life falls into focus.

Father, give to us beyond the joys of human companionship the precious knowledge of thy presence.

JUNE 6. *Pray for us: for we trust we have a good conscience, in all things willing to live honestly.* —HEBREWS 13:18

Friends who are united in the bonds of prayer have a power which transcends separation when paths inevitably take their individual routes, and which helps heal in time of illness or great sorrow. Integrated with this prayer power must be the willingness to live honestly, whatever the daily routine. This basic honesty seems to help channel effective prayer.

Father, we are willing to live honestly, but often we are weak in the face of temptation. Please strengthen our wills.

JUNE 7. *For the Lord seeth not as man seeth; for man looketh on the outward appearance, but the Lord looketh on the heart.*—I SAMUEL 16:7

Marriage counselors feel that often June marriages fall into disrepair because the young bride was more concerned with the ruffles of the trousseau than with the inner qualities of the man she was to marry. Often he is bruised when he discovers her sweetness was as artificial as perfume. A part of successful marriage involves looking on the inner qualities of the heart, which are important to happy permanence.

Loving Father, give us a greater sense of thy understanding that we may see aright in our daily contacts.

JUNE 8. *Therefore, my brethren dearly beloved and longed for, my joy and crown, so stand fast in the Lord, my dearly beloved.*—PHILIPPIANS 4:1

A phrase precious to the hearts of many is that which begins some marriage services—"Dearly beloved." It has its origin in the Bible as an expression of mutual love among the disciples, and with it goes an obligation. We who are thus dearly beloved must learn to "stand fast in the Lord," holding onto the virtues we have learned about and trying to put them to active use in marriage, housework, or business contacts.

Father, because we share the fellowship of the dearly beloved, let us grow in grace and in a stronger knowledge of thy love.

JUNE 9. *Wash me thoroughly from mine iniquity, and cleanse me from my sin.*—PSALM 51:2

With the happy appearance of the garden in June, there is often the flash of bird wings through the spray from the garden hose. Even the little creatures of the woods come to the edge of the natural pool to wash themselves free of the sand and dust. Inherent in each of us is the wish to be made clean, and this can happen through confession and faith.

Father, for the joys of June make us ready with clean hearts, washed pure in the healing streams of thy unfailing love.

JUNE 10. *For the love of money is the root of all evil.*—I TIMOTHY 6:10

None of us likes to be interrupted from the enjoyment of natural beauty or the fellowship of friends to have to think about money. Yet the tenth of the month rolls around, and bills must be paid, including those for wedding gifts and bridal showers. Young couples fall into difficulty because they have not considered how money shall be spent. The Bible counsels against the evil of loving money as an end in itself.

Father, help us to learn to share the little we have so that we may have receptive minds for the more thou wilt give to us.

JUNE 11. *To the Lord our God belong mercies and forgivenesses, though we have rebelled against him.* —DANIEL 9:9

Sometimes quarrels descend into a family with the suddenness of a June thunder shower, forcing hearts to run for cover as do guests at a garden party. Thus it is important for schoolmates to learn understanding and forgiveness of the faults of their young friends. Certainly brides and grooms find it important to learn the art of forgiveness at an early date. Ultimately all forgiveness belongs to God, who knows our human frailties.

Father, forgive us as we would be forgiven, and help us to learn the difficult art of forgiving those who hurt us.

JUNE 12. *Behold, God is my salvation; I will trust, and not be afraid.*—ISAIAH 12:2

111

It is a paradox of life that joy and sorrow seem to be two sides of the same coin. So it is that any month which contains so much of happiness as does June may in later years be the source of memories which come back through tears. If the heart is fighting the loneliness of losing a loved one by death or the strange circumstances of modern living, this is the time to rely on the everlasting promises of God, the father.

Lord, help us to be not afraid, no matter what unexpected situations may be presented to us in modern civilization.

JUNE 13. *Who is a wise man and endued with knowledge among you? let him shew out of a good conversation his works with meekness of wisdom.—* JAMES 3:13

Commencement speeches concern themselves with the meaning of wisdom, often quoting from the ancients. No better definition has been given than these words from the Bible, which combine meekness with wisdom. For the mind which remains humble can always be filled with fresh truth, and the truly wise individual keeps his conversation good with helpful words of compassion and understanding.

God, keep us from the burden of thinking we know it all, but let us be in a position to receive fresh truth from thee.

JUNE 14. *Now we exhort you, brethren, warn them that are unruly, comfort the feebleminded, support the weak, be patient toward all men.*—I THESSALONIANS 5:14

Much complicated advice can be summarized into this code of action, which seems pointed toward the current age marked by violence. Since there are unruly people of all ages intent on overthrowing much that is good as well as changing the bad, this is a time which demands great quantities of patience. Through the exercise of such virtue it is possible to help those whose own faith may be weak. This is no time to be feeble.

Father, we give our weaknesses into thy strength, asking thee to grant patience moment by moment through busy days.

JUNE 15. *Nor height, nor depth, nor any other creature, shall be able to separate us from the love of God, which is in Christ Jesus our Lord.*—ROMANS 8:39

What comfort and consolation there are in these precious words. They are especially helpful when young people leave for military service, or when there is a traffic accident, and perhaps the body of a loved one must be returned home for burial. If in life and death we feel that nothing can separate us from the love of God, we have strength and power which no formal education can ever grant, and no human lover or friend can give or take away from our hearts.

Father, in this uncertain life, we give thee thanks for the certainties of the scripture, which we claim as our own.

JUNE 16. *The grass withereth, the flower fadeth: but the word of our God shall stand for ever.*—ISAIAH 40:8

One of the chores of June is taking down the floral decorations after lovely affairs of sentiment. Perhaps it is dismantling the daisy chain following commencement, or removing the dainty nosegays of pink and white carnations from the ends of church pews following a wedding. In such moments of nostalgia it is apparent that flowers do fade swiftly. Blessed is the happy heart which knows that God's love is ever the same.

Father, help us to hold anew each day the precious promises of thy eternal love and everlasting help to thy children.

JUNE 17. *Correct thy son, and he shall give thee rest; yea, he shall give delight unto thy soul.*—PROVERBS 29:17

Along about the middle of June, many parents gain a new respect for schoolteachers, as the "vacation jitters" come into families. Released from regular schedules, children often wonder what to do next, and sometimes this curiosity leads to practices which must be curbed early in the season. When discipline is needed the parent may suffer more than the child, but necessary correction can develop a delightful person.

God, we look back upon times when life has chastised us because we were not reacting properly, and we give thee belated thanks.

JUNE 18. *The Lord is my strength and my shield; my heart trusted in him, and I am helped.*—PSALM 28:7

When new problems arrive with new seasons, sometimes it is hard to know which way to decide. Shall the family proceed to drive across country to visit grandparents, or would it be better for a small son to remain at home to take needed school credits in the summer session? These can be questions which divide the heart. No matter is too trivial to take in prayer to God asking for help in creating a happy summer situation.

God, for the beautiful opportunities for fellowship and learning, accept our thanks and help us use them wisely.

JUNE 19. *Know ye not that ye are the temple of God, and that the Spirit of God dwelleth in you?*—I CORINTHIANS 3:16

How soft and cool the grass feels beneath bare feet in June, whether one is walking in the yard or getting ready to dive into a swimming pool. Summer brings a fresh awareness of the human body. Sometimes there is the wish to take off pounds or put on more through the weeks of vacation. Doctors say this is best accomplished when emotional problems are surrendered. When spirit and body are in harmony, much progress can be made toward good health in that marvelous mechanism, the human body.

Father, help us to make our own bodies strong that we may have health for the tasks of our generation involving others.

JUNE 20. *Heal me, O Lord, and I shall be healed; save me, and I shall be saved; for thou art my praise.* —JEREMIAH 17:14

A new development in recent years is the growth of camps given over to children with special diabetic problems or handicaps of limb or sight. Fellowship with children in like situations has a therapeutic effect, particularly when there is cheerful leadership. Sometimes this encouragement will help the child increase his own courage and work harder to develop good health habits. Healing may come through happy fellowship.

God, heal us through the divine ministry of outdoor blessings of summer, as we relax to receive thee more fully into our lives.

JUNE 21. *With long life will I satisfy him, and shew him my salvation.*—PSALM 91:16

On this longest day of the current calendar year, we awake with an appreciation of the light which lingers into night, and we are often aware of how short are the years and life itself. Even in the days of the Psalmist there was a longing for length of life, but even more for enduring satisfactions. These are definitely promised to those who learn to trust God and dwell with him through the long and short days of life.

Father, let our days be long in service, and short in complaining, so that we may learn the deep satisfactions of living.

JUNE 22. *Then touched he their eyes, saying, According to your faith be it unto you.*—MATTHEW 9:29

In a long ago summertime a grandparent gave to a little boy a microscope. So a scientist explained his lifelong dedication to learning which had led to unusual discoveries about God's universe. With the glass in hand, the little boy had examined the ants in his own backyard, looked at the veins on the leaf in the tree which held the swing. Never had he felt deprived because he could not travel, for the world was all around him. Each June offers a new opportunity to look closely at beauty.

God, forgive us the great sin of not being aware of what is nearest to us, and help us grow in clarity of vision.

JUNE 23. *The cloak that I left at Troas with Carpus, when thou comest, bring with thee, and the books, but especially the parchments.*—II TIMOTHY 4:13

The love of books can make any period of vacation or of enforced rest because of illness or accident a time of great growth. Here is one of the most human verses of the New Testament, where the apostle Paul asks wistfully for his books, expressing an especial fondness for the "parchments." In many families such a beautiful piece of lettering on old parchment is cherished. How wonderful is the more leisurely pace of summer for reading enjoyment!

God, grant us happy moments of learning more about thy truth and how to express learning in modern day action.

JUNE 24. *Remove far from me vanity and lies: give me neither poverty nor riches; feed me with food convenient for me.*—PROVERBS 30:8

In the simplicities of summer lie much happiness, for vanity can be kept at a minimum in informal living and easy entertainment. This is a happy period in which the joys of munching a sandwich can be savored beneath the stars while a neighbor contributes a cookie made from a cherished recipe. In the open-hearted sharing of summer potluck suppers there is an opportunity to come to know people better, and to just enjoy family and friends.

Father, too often we look at riches and poverty from afar, not realizing we are rich in thee, and poor in our acceptance.

JUNE 25. *Let them praise his name in the dance: let them sing praises unto him with the timbrel and harp.*—PSALM 149:3

In setting up a summer schedule there is opportunity to plan ahead for some nice musical or dance program which the children will remember for a long time. It may also restore memories to their parents of when they were freer to attend such concerts. Looking forward to such a treat in a nearby city, or even buying a new record for the family can give fresh zest to a humdrum summer. Simple pleasures can lead to happiness and praise.

119

Father, we are grateful for the opportunity to sing praises and to rejoice in thy goodness to thy children.

JUNE 26. *As a bird that wandereth from her nest, so is a man that wandereth from his place.*—PROVERBS 27:8

A bird which is late in its migratory pattern finds trouble locating food and water. Children in summer sometimes find such stragglers and attempt to tame them. When the bird receives some fresh strength or a wing is repaired, it may beat frantically against the cage asking release to fly again in the blue sky. Fortunately the man or woman who has lost the way in life can be restored from wandering by a return to faith and trust.

Father, the yearly pressures of life bear in upon us, and we would use the blessed summer months to find our way to thee.

JUNE 27. *Ye are my friends, if ye do whatsoever I command you.*—JOHN 15:14

What a scurrying of dusting and rearranging furniture often occurs when a letter arrives saying an old friend will be stopping by for a summer visit. There is something special in that word "friend" which means the restoring of a happy relationship of understanding. Often friends speak the same words at the same instant, or read ahead what is in the heart of the other. Significantly Jesus used this treasured word in welcoming his disciples to his side for all time.

Father, we would indeed live as we are commanded, so that we may know the true meaning of friendship with thee.

JUNE 28. *And that was counted unto him for righteousness unto all generations for evermore.*—PSALM 106:31

There is something ageless about the hills with their huge rocks and giant stream beds. Similarly some stories of bravery within the family circle carry through from one generation of young people to the next. The stories which endure have something of the stability of the rocks, and flow like a fresh stream of truth encouraging others to try to live with nobility. This is a good season to refresh the heart with stories of courage.

God, help us in our little days of trivial tasks to try to serve with courage, so that we become a part of righteous living.

JUNE 29. *But to whom little is forgiven, the same loveth little.*—LUKE 7:47

121

Awkward situations may arise in setting up summer guest lists, for not everybody feels the same sense of rapport. Some indeed find it almost impossible to ever forgive a real or fancied slight and seem to love to carry grudges against those who are willing to be friends. If there is heaviness in your heart in dealing with acquaintances, this is a good time to forgive and to forget the past in happy fellowship of the present.

Father, we would love thee more in gratitude for the times in which we have been forgiven. Help us to extend this boon to others.

JUNE 30. *Trust in the Lord with all thine heart; and lean not unto thine own understanding.*—PROVERBS 3:5

All of us long for adventures. Yet we sometimes hesitate to try to make new friends, or even to go to a different place for a family vacation. We feel safer in clinging to old possessions and the past. Yet the Bible admonishes that we are to look beyond such tangible things, and to trust the Lord and his understanding, which is sufficient for all new situations, happy or sad, as the seasons progress.

God, give to us all a sense of adventure and companionship whether we travel to far places or serve thee at home.

July

LORD OF LIBERTY, WE THANK THEE
FOR FREEDOM TO LIVE OUR LIVES AS
HAPPY CHILDREN OF THINE. MAY WE
SHOW OUR APPRECIATION IN WHOLE-
SOME FAMILY LIVING AND AS GOOD
CITIZENS.

JULY 1. *Stand fast therefore in the liberty wherewith Christ hath made us free, and be not entangled again with the yoke of bondage.*—GALATIANS 5:1

With the first half of the year behind us, there is a renewed impetus to make the most of the summer months ahead. We feel freer to live informally, with some of the routine meetings dropped from club and church schedules. With this should come a happier, lighter feeling that we may always be free to enjoy the most of the best gifts which God has provided for those who love and serve him.

Dear God, keep us from becoming slaves of pettiness and actions unworthy of thy children, cherishing our freedom in Christ.

JULY 2. *And Jesus answered and said unto her, Martha, Martha, thou art careful and troubled about many things.*—LUKE 10:41

This answer is so familiar that everybody seems to know the question which preceded it—the common complaint of being too busy. The summer schedule looms large with many extra details for mothers involved in getting clothing ready for summer camps, or planning for an annual family reunion over the forthcoming holiday. The wise words of Jesus speak to crowded schedules. Do you really need to do everything you have planned for this summer day?

Father, help us to hold to the happy planning at the base of our busy lives and not to get lost in the execution of details.

JULY 3. *Be strong, and quit yourselves like men . . . quit yourselves like men, and fight.*—I SAMUEL 4:9

As the anniversary of our nation's birthday approaches, there is great sadness in the hearts of those who have lost loved ones in the many conflicts since the first Independence Day. It is then that the advice given since time immemorial to fighters needs to be taken into the hearts of even the most delicate and feminine members of the family circle. In these days of crisis, each of us must fight the evils of the spirit, even as our gallant fighting men.

God, we would be strong in facing our losses, and we ask for strength from thee to bear the burdens of this age of change.

JULY 4. *Awake, awake, put on strength, O arm of the Lord; awake, as in the ancient days, in the generations of old.*—ISAIAH 51:9

Brilliant sunshine in a bright blue sky calls families out of doors on this glorious day of remembrance. Perhaps it is traditional to have a picnic with friends and relatives, or to join in a community celebration climaxed at night by fireworks near the lake. From pioneer days, the birthday of our nation has been a time to think about spiritual strength and to become awake to opportunities for service and fellowship.

Father, we thank thee for our gracious heritage, and we ask for wisdom to preserve it in righteousness for the new generation.

JULY 5. *Keep thy tongue from evil, and thy lips from speaking guile.*—PSALM 34:13

On the morning after the Fourth of July holiday, the newspaper columns are full of oratory and reprints of speeches made in the name of democracy and patriotism. Sometimes a fresh phrase will give new meaning to the old virtues of unselfish sharing and dedication to the common interest. Even these beautiful new words are meaningless unless they are prompted by sincerity, and unless the tongue is matched by willing hands at work.

Father, give us a sense of perspective that we may speak words of truth for right action.

JULY 6. *And he that reapeth receiveth wages, and gathereth fruit unto life eternal: that both he that soweth and he that reapeth may rejoice together.*—JOHN 4:36

It is a high point in the life of any youngster in the family when he first receives a summer job. This may be baby-sitting for the neighbor's children, or a handsome teen-ager may get the job of teaching swimming in a nearby pool. It is a wonderful moment when any individual learns the joy of working for wages, even as the employer is glad to find someone to perform efficient service for stated sums. The right attitude about work and wages makes for daily joy.

Father, keep us in tune with thee as we work happily at various projects in thy interesting world.

JULY 7. *Cause me to hear thy loving-kindness in the morning; for in thee do I trust.*—PSALM 143:8

Summertime brings an awareness of youth and the morning time of life. Perhaps this becomes evident when a toddler comes walking onto the grass, and we realize this is the child who had to be carried in arms even as recently as the last holiday season. Or a bronzed college lad stops by briefly en route to a new job assignment or on his way to military service. In the beauty of summer mornings there is a chance to accept again the daily opportunities for trusting in God and keeping the spirit of youth.

Father, let these summer days be ones of fellowship with our loved ones and with thee, as fresh blessings come with each morning.

JULY 8. *I had fainted, unlesss I had believed to see the goodness of the Lord in the land of the living.*—PSALM 27:13

The sharp jangle of the telephone often changes happy vacation plans. The call may summon parents to the emergency room at the hospital because a child has fallen from his bicycle. All thought of the planned camping trip is pushed aside, as the family prays for the child's recovery. In all such emergencies the precious promises of Bible truth can sustain and undergird anxious days of waiting for restored health.

God, we are often fainthearted, but we trust in thy goodness and ask for thy help in meeting all of life's demands.

JULY 9. *Till he fill thy mouth with laughing, and thy lips with rejoicing.*—JOB 8:21

A simple word like "till" or "until" can do much to keep the mind focused on a better future. If we can just wait until the mail arrives today, there may be good news from home or the soldier son away in service. Should it not come there may be momentary sadness, but this can be dispelled in thinking about the possible arrival of a phone call, or surely tomorrow's mail. Any summer is happier because of its "untils."

Father, we want our portion of laughter and rejoicing, and we are grateful for thy fellowship waiting until fulfillment.

JULY 10. *And forgive us our debts, as we forgive our debtors.*—MATTHEW 6:12

128

In business offices, this is often one of the heaviest working days of the month. Likewise some housewives find it a difficult one in writing checks and deciding budgets. In homes where there is not an efficient system of managing funds, this may prove a day of quarreling as various members of the family try to justify their special expenses. A hunger for new things often results in temper strain when it comes time to pay just debts. Loving money and its products must be tempered by love of family.

Father, if there have been hard words about wishes and debts, help us to forgive and to use better judgment in planning ahead.

JULY 11. *I will freely sacrifice unto thee: I will praise thy name, O Lord; for it is good.*—PSALM 54:6

Every parent knows the joy of sacrificing for a child who longs for a special gift, whether this be a new red dress with white polka dots or a special sweater at camp. It becomes easier to do without magazines or a new kitchen utensil if one thinks of the smile on the face of the youngster, who in turn must learn to give up in behalf of others. The sacrifice made freely is the one which brings the happiest blessing and rejoices the heart of God.

Father, we are glad for the chance to learn something of thy sacrifice for us when we share ourselves with our loved one-

JULY 12. *There is sorrow on the sea; it cannot be quiet.*—JEREMIAH 49:23

For many families, summer begins with an annual trip to the nearby river or pond. If the home is located near the coast it surely includes that first seasonal visit to the seashore. There is a fascination in watching the waters, endlessly moving in ceaseless waves, ever coming to the sandy, rocky shoreline and then returning to the deep. This is the way of life, and in its essential ebb and flo there is momentary sadness, but joy in the fact that we all are part of God's swelling tide.

Father, for our common humanity accept our thanks, as we reflect on the beauty of thy natural universe with its restless sea.

JULY 13. *I will lift up mine eyes unto the hills, from whence cometh my help.*—PSALM 121:1

On the happy morning when the family started on vacation, the mother said, "I'll see my mountain again." She referred to the picture kept in the kitchen. It was an enlarged snapshot which showed the peak near the family campground. All year long as she peeled potatoes, placed a gingerbread in the oven, or removed the roast, she had quick glimpses of the mountain which the family enjoyed together. Such memories and anticipation made routine tasks easier to accomplish.

God, grant us daily joy as we climb the hills of hope and walk the paths of trust in meeting our daily schedules.

JULY 14. *And take the helmet of salvation, and the sword of the Spirit, which is the word of God.*— EPHESIANS 6:17

Packing for any vacation involves spreading many items out on the floor of the living room or garage, and then determining what can be left behind. Some fathers have been known to believe that the family thinks the car is made of rubber and can stretch to hold tennis rackets, doll cribs, or a bed for the family pet. Inevitably something must be discarded. This is true also in the journey of life where one irreplaceable item is the word of God.

Father, we take different journeys in various ways, but each of us needs the refreshment which comes from thy holy word.

JULY 15. *And he said, Whereunto shall we liken the kingdom of God? or with what comparison shall we compare it?*—MARK 4:30

Standing on the rim of the Grand Canyon, or looking up to the towering peaks in Alaska or Europe, the tourist

131

often says, "There are no words to describe what I see and what I feel." This is also the sentiment of the heart which takes time to think about the kingdom of God, for there is nothing to which it can be compared in beauty, once it is experienced in a personal way. This can become a highpoint of this particular summer.

Father, we are grateful that we may share the wonderful beauty of thy eternal kingdom.

JULY 16. *The lines are fallen unto me in pleasant places; yea, I have a goodly heritage.*—PSALM 16:6

White fleecy clouds in a bright blue sky burnished by the golden sun of July make a perfect setting for a leisurely summer day of visiting. Sometimes this date falls on a Sunday when relatives may be invited home for fried chicken and mashed potatoes and apple pie with vanilla ice cream. Again it may be a working day when memories of such fellowship bless routine tasks and one is aware that home is indeed a pleasant place with a goodly heritage to cherish.

God, keep us aware of our blessings while we have them, and let us enjoy them always in sacred memories.

JULY 17. *And they departed into a desert place by ship privately.*—MARK 6:32

Hot summer days are not conducive to desert crossings. During this season vacationers usually plan to travel by night in the hot sandy areas. Then the stars are brilliant and seem close enough to touch through the open window of the automobile. In Bible times the word "desert" meant any place of aloneness, where there was opportunity for meditation. This is the desired goal of true recreation even today—to find a place where we may indeed possess our own souls.

Father, may there be some time allocated to each of us for that which will refresh us most, preparing us for service.

JULY 18. *In the shadow of his hand hath he hid me.*
—ISAIAH 49:2

Even the birds seek for shade in this hot month of summer, sometimes resting within the shadow of a fluttering leaf, casting its figure shape on the green lawn. All creatures long for shade to help restore them from the heat of the blazing sun. It is a comfort to many hearts in the days of struggle and crisis over national and international problems to know that God provides shade and strength.

God, keep us alert and marching in the sun to solve problems, because we gain rest in the shadow of thy love.

JULY 19. *A time to weep and a time to laugh . . .*
—ECCLESIASTES 3:4

In the long evenings of summer, the laughter of little children can often be heard for a long distance. Sometimes it even seems too loud to adults who want to rest from a day's work, or who come in with fresh fish to clean from the vacation's successful trip to the stream or beach. The echoes of laughter sound not only on the day of the jest and pleasure, but remain in the heart as precious memories. Summer is the time to tie memories with the golden garland of laughter.

God, we thank thee for placing laughter into thy world, and we want to keep the gift of laughter in our hearts each day.

JULY 20. *No man also seweth a piece of new cloth on an old garment: else the new piece that filled it up taketh away from the old, and the rent is made worse.*
—MARK 2:21

When the work basket is filled with accumulated mending it becomes time to go into the coolest room of the house or out under a tree and tackle the letting out of blouses, or the changing of hems on skirts. It is then the housewife learns again the wisdom of many of the Bible parables, based on homely truths. For there is a moment

134

when a garment cannot be made to fit current needs and must be discarded, even as outmoded ideas must change to fit the new generations.

God, we want to hold to all that is good, but we pray for flexible minds so that we may accept necessary changes for progress.

JULY 21. *For the ways of the Lord are right, and the just shall walk in them: but the transgressor shall fall therein*—HOSEA 14:9

Walking in the woods on vacation, there comes an inevitable time when decision must be reached as to which way to turn at the fork of the road. This experience is repeated daily in modern life as individuals face election problems, or wonder which house to buy or where to invest funds wisely. In all such decisions, help is available from God who offers the way which is "right" to the just who follow his commandments.

God, when we are tempted to turn aside from what we feel is the right way, help us to keep from falling through transgression.

JULY 22. *But he himself went a day's journey into the wilderness, and came and sat down under a juniper tree.*
—I KINGS 19:4

So familiar is the rest of this verse that the mere mention of the juniper tree usually conjures up in the mind of the listener the feeling of the depression which marked the heart, and which is memoralized in song. No matter how happy is the summer, there comes a moment of discouragement, perhaps based on tiredness from hiking, or cooking over a makeshift stove without home conveniences. All of us need to sit down alone under the juniper tree occasionally and wait for the renewal of strength, and should not be ashamed of these lapses from our usual cheerful good nature.

God, from temporary or longer depression, may there come greater knowledge of thee and thy loving kindnesses to us.

JULY 23. *If any of you lack wisdom, let him ask of God, that giveth to all men liberally, and upbraideth not; and it shall be given him.*—JAMES 1:5

A prominent psychologist claims that the trouble with many of his patients is that they are unwilling to ask for help. The first step in their progress to normal behavior is the willingness to receive that which is available to help them turn from melancholy to restored activity in daily routine. Even those of us who may escape psychiatric help find it hard on occasion to ask God for the help he is so willing to give.

136

Father, forgive our stubborn independence, and help us to know that thou art always ready to give when we ask thee.

JULY 24. *Happy is the man that feareth alway: but he that hardeneth his heart shall fall into mischief.* —PROVERBS 28:14

Echoing on the evening air came the taunt from the baseball game, "You are just an old softie." The youngest child on the field seemed afraid that the ball would hit him. Constantly he moved away instead of stepping in to receive the ball. The teasing of his playmates only increased his nervousness. He was finding it difficult to achieve the proper balance between hardness and softness. This is something each of us must learn for wise living.

Father, we want to be happy and keep our normal fears under control, avoiding the brittleness of hardness and mischief.

JULY 25. *I have blotted out, as a thick cloud, thy transgressions, and, as a cloud, thy sins: return unto me; for I have redeemed thee.*—ISAIAH 44:22

Swiftly the summer clouds blot out the sunshine, and a thick cloud may cover the earth so that rain seems imminent. It is an awesome moment in any summer day when there is this abrupt change. It can come as quickly into any heart which surrenders its sins and temptations to God, who has the power to blot transgressions from the heart, even as he controls the clouds over the sun. No summer needs to be made unhappy by repression and guilt which can be changed.

God, we lose sight of thy power to blot out the past, and just now we ask thee to make the present worthy of eternity.

JULY 26. *And the people stood afar off, and Moses drew near unto the thick darkness where God was.* —Exodus 20:21

Watching a lightning bug in the darkness of a hot summer night is a never-ending fascination to children. It is one of the joys which carries over from past generations into the future. Perhaps this family enjoyment of the simple little bug grows out of the human wish for light in darkness. The Bible promises that even in thick darkness God is present.

Father, sometimes we must wait in what seems like great personal darkness, and we are glad to know thou art there, too.

JULY 27. *Howbeit the most High dwelleth not in temples made with hands; as saith the prophet.*—ACTS 7:48

Vacation visits to temples do not need to be confined to far places of the world. Many communities join together in summer services of worship, sharing various local "temples" with those of other faiths. Whether the edifice is large and memorable, like one we discover in travel, or small and simple, the occasion is important because of the feeling of worship. This is available also in God's great out of doors, as his spirit permeates life.

God, help us take occasions for renewal of the spirit in all the experiences of this summertime.

JULY 28. *Being then made free from sin, ye became the servants of righteousness.*—ROMANS 6:18

From the trees at the far corner of the lawn came the voices of the children in mild quarreling. One said to her brother, "Pray tell, who was your servant last year?" and his reply was lost in the muffled scuffling as the tiff was forgotten. None of us likes to be a servant, and so we naturally fight the necessity to become servants of righteousness, serving in our generation for the causes of good. The Bible counsels that this responsibility follows forgiveness of sins.

139

Father, help us fight our native selfishness, losing it in happy-hearted service for others and thee.

JULY 29. *Every valley shall be filled, and every mountain and hill shall be brought low; and the crooked shall be made straight, and the rough ways shall be made smooth.*—LUKE 3:5

Traveling cross-country the visitor constantly encounters evidences of road changes. What was once a steep, winding, rugged mountain road may have become a six-lane super-highway as giants made of steel have cut through the dirt and granite to make a substantial roadbed. All this speeds up travel and makes it safer. The Bible promises something of this engineering of the heart as God has power even to turn the rough ways into smooth paths through his love.

Father, when the hills overwhelm us, help us to cling to the assurance that thou hast prepared a true pathway for our hearts.

JULY 30. *Fill ye up then the measure of your fathers.*—MATTHEW 23:32

With dismay the father turned off the radio which was bringing news of accidents, slaughter through war, and bickering at high counsel tables. "I'd like to tune out the human race," he said in deep disgust, and many of us know how he felt. Yet in our hearts we know that there is a continuing obligation to bind up the wounds of the injured, and to keep trying to find the way to peace. The Bible indicates that the new generation must even do what the past failed to accomplish.

God, we would not shirk our duty, but we need more help from thee in our homes, businesses, and through all our associations.

JULY 31. *And I will give him the morning star.*
—REVELATION 2:28

What is more wonderful than to recall the summer morning when as a child at the window you had a first glimpse of the morning star. Perhaps it was when a grandparent took a lad on his first fishing excursion, or the family started for a mountain camping trip. This simple pleasure may be granted the new generation in this particular summer. We all need to look up into the clear sky of early morning as a fresh day begins, to be reminded that the stars remain as the weeks and months go by swiftly.

Father, for the joys of this month which is drawing to a close accept our thanks, and help us set new aims of accomplishment.

August

DEAR GOD OF SUMMER'S DAYS, MAY
WE KNOW ANEW THE COMFORT OF
ETERNAL FELLOWSHIP WITH THEE BE-
NEATH THE STARS OR WALKING IN
MEADOWS BESIDE THE STREAMS. KEEP
US AWARE OF THY GREAT CARE.

AUGUST 1. *And when ye see the south wind blow, ye say, There will be heat; and it cometh to pass.—* LUKE 12:55

There is a certain look of the sky when August appears on the calendar, and there is a feel about the wind which promises a hot day. These simple signs we learn to read after living in an area for any length of time, and the prudent housewife will shut the windows early to keep in the night air for coolness. Likewise, there are signs

142

which identify the loving heart which helps to bear the heat and burdens of the day, for such people look for ways to give the cooling balm of fellowship to others.

Father, help us to adapt to the experiences of the summer of life in ways which show we are followers of thy will.

AUGUST 2. *I know thy works, that thou art neither cold nor hot: I would thou wert cold or hot.*—REVELATION 3:15

The man who tends lawns during summer vacations once confided to the neighborhood, "Even though it gets so awfully hot when you people are away, I like to work. The heat bakes away some of my aches and meanness." Not everybody shares his feeling, but all of us seem to like genuineness, whether this involves heat or cold, light or dark. It is a wonderful blessing when we encounter a friend who is genuine in all the experiences of living, and whose warmth of understanding is enduring.

God, keep us from being indefinite in our witnessing, but let us develop positive attitudes of warmhearted interest.

AUGUST 3. *Let them be as grass upon the housetops, which withereth afore it groweth up.*—PSALM 129:6

A summer pastime of many children is the making of playhouses in tree tops, some of which are given attractive grass roofs. How cool and pleasant they seem on the first day or two! But soon the grass withers, and the youngsters must replace it or use a tarpaper substitute, or find another plaything. Often pleasures seem as attractive as the grass roof when encountered as vacation temptations, but they wither in the light of the individual's true character and integrity.

Father, keep our dreams and our idealism from withering before there is time for growth and achievement.

AUGUST 4. *Distributing to the necessity of saints; given to hospitality.*—ROMANS 12:13

With the relaxed days of August it would seem that households might find more rest than during the busy school year, but often there are many extra chores because of visitors. City relatives come to the country, or those from mountain areas descend upon friends at the beaches. Hospitality calls for hard work on the part of someone. Each of us can learn to be a useful guest in the world, carrying our proportionate share of life's load.

Father, help us accept the opportunity for summer fellowship by learning to be good hosts and good guests enjoying life.

AUGUST 5. *Thus saith the Lord, Set thine house in order; for thou shalt die, and not live.*—II KINGS 20:1

A chore facing many households in summer is that of cleaning the closet which has been a depository for old magazines, books, clippings, and seasonal decorations. We look forward to a block of time in which to take care of this often neglected chore. None of us likes to face the further fact that we should put our wills in order, and recognize that someday we will not be here to enjoy our possessions. The Bible is a book of realism which counsels us to take practical action.

Father, give us grace to face the facts of life and death and measure up to the need to put our house of life in order.

AUGUST 6. *A man that hath friends must shew himself friendly: and there is a friend that sticketh closer than a brother.*—PROVERBS 18:24

Planning to meet an old friend for lunch in the vacation month of August can prove a seasonal highlight. Schedules get busy with the workaday routine, and years can go by without such a pleasant visit unless a day is set and circled on the calendar. This simple act is one way to show friendliness and can result in remembered pleasure through all the year. Likewise it is necessary to plan ahead for time in divine companionship through a meeting in prayer and meditation which brings blessings.

Father, whatever happens in life, help us to keep on friendly terms with thee and with thy children we meet each day.

AUGUST 7. *He that loveth his brother abideth in the light, and there is none occasion of stumbling in him.* —I JOHN 2:10

A practice in some areas in the hot summer months is to pull down the blinds, so that bright August sunlight does not add to the heat of the house. Yet there is something gloomy about such a room, and it is a good moment when at last the blinds are raised to let in the light and the afternoon breezes. So it is a good experience when love cancels out gloom and welcomes a friend as a brother. It takes the light of love to keep from stumbling in darkness or loneliness.

God, even though we may need to withdraw into temporary shade, restore us so we may abide in light and love.

AUGUST 8. *Now the God of patience and consolation grant you to be likeminded one toward another according to Christ Jesus.*—ROMAN: 15:5

146

With children playing in the yard, or visitors arriving for a weekend, the housewife feels the need of patience on hot days. It is easy to scream and yell for quiet, thus adding to the noise and confusion of the vacation schedule. What should be a happy, carefree time becomes an involved one. If it is to be enjoyed by all, there is need for patience. This is found in a quiet moment of contemplation even in the midst of pressing chores and duties. Each of us can afford to stop what we are doing for one moment and wait for patience.

Lord, let us not crowd so much into minutes, hours, and days that we miss the joys of like-minded fellowship and patience.

AUGUST 9. *He turneth the wilderness into a standing water, and dry ground into watersprings.*—PSALM 107:35

One of the endless chores of summer is the watering of the garden. If there are to be bright red zinnias as a border to the entryway, or waxy string beans to pop and thread for dinner, the watering must be continued at early morning or in the evening so that the sun does not evaporate the moisture. The family sometimes longs for a spring which will keep the dry ground wet and productive. The heart is promised this blessing for its barrenness through trust in the wellsprings of God.

Father, we meet with dry spells in our living, and we ask thee humbly for the water of life to keep our hearts pure.

AUGUST 10. *Be watchful, and strengthen the things which remain, that are ready to die: for I have not found thy works perfect before God.*—REVELATION 3:2

Planning for vacation, one is shocked to discover that some of the money planned for the gasoline and hotel has been used up in clothing and recreation equipment. There comes a time when the family budget must be watched, so that joyous experiences do not have to be obliterated from the family vacation. None of us is perfect in our financial planning, but any of us can learn to "strengthen the things which remain"—and this includes the growth of love for each member of the family, sharing together.

Father, keep us from selfishness, whether this involves money or hobbies, and let us learn to strengthen one another.

AUGUST 11. *And Mizpah; for he said, the Lord watch between me and thee, when we are absent one from another.*—Genesis 31:49

A verse which has been quoted over the years has new meanings in fresh situations. The word "Mizpah" itself has come to be spiritual shorthand for a promise in parting. Many are such separations in the month of August, whether these involve saying good-bye to an aged parent after a visit at the family home, or waving to a son leaving by airplane for his military service abroad, or to a young child on a bus for summer camp. God's presence bridges such separations.

Father, we need thee every hour, and are aware of this keenly when transient earthly separations strain our emotions.

AUGUST 12. *The sun shall not smite thee by day, nor the moon by night.*—PSALM 121:6

Beating down on the garden walk at noontime, the sunlight seems bright indeed, and on an August night of the full moon the light seems bright as day. As friends and family linger over a picnic in the patio it is hard to realize that the ancients needed to be reassured that moonlight and sunlight would not "smite" them. Instead the promise of God's word is always for happy fulfillment, and there is abiding joy in the brilliant light of summer days and evenings, meant for happy-hearted fellowship.

Father, we do enjoy thy blessings of beauty, and thank thee that they are universal over our homes in all localities.

AUGUST 13.   *For a small moment have I forsaken thee; but with great mercies will I gather thee.—* ISAIAH 54:7

It is impossible to escape a feeling of nostalgia at some time during the heat of summer. Perhaps the day itself produces a feeling of listlessness which reminds one of days of more vigorous health when it was possible to swim long distances in the pool. Maybe the day marks an anniversary of a wedding, with one of the partners now gone, or perhaps the expected letter fails to arrive from overseas. All depression should be treated as the "small moment" ahead of the gathering of mercies.

Father, we are sorry when depressions blot out the joys ahead, and we would have them removed as swiftly as summer storms.

AUGUST 14.   *Let your moderation be known unto all men. The Lord is at hand.—*PHILIPPIANS 4:5

Physicians advise us that one of the ways to keep well and happy in the summertime is to be moderate in all things. Too much exercising in the hot sun can bring on physical difficulties, but it is also true that too little can lead to lassitude. Moderation in matters of the emotions can also help to make hot days more bearable. To avoid excesses is good counsel at any time of year, but can be cultivated to extraordinary effectiveness if practiced as the thermometer climbs.

Father, we are impatient and often immoderate in both thinking and action. Help us to learn moderation.

AUGUST 15. *A faithful man shall abound with blessings.*—PROVERBS 28:20

When the family next door left for vacation, they asked the neighbor boy if he would water the lawn and flowers, and feed the dog and cat. Excitedly the child promised a happy "Yes," for this was his first job. It was not always easy to come in from riding his bicycle at the right time to complete his tasks, but he was faithful each day. The returning neighbors were so pleased that they offered him a weekly job in their garden. Faithfulness takes many forms and always contains blessings.

Father, we would be faithful to thee and to the best that we know, always learning more of this blessing.

AUGUST 16. *And a man shall be . . . as rivers of water in a dry place, as the shadow of a great rock in a weary land.*—ISAIAH 32:2

These precious words applicable to a month calling for water and shadows refer to a man of righteousness. They are applicable today to the friends who provide help in time of need. About such people there is an aura of beauty, similar to that seen in the great Southwest, when large rocks make their interesting shadows on the desert sands, so that even the cattle walk toward the image of coolness. Each of us throws a shadow of influence toward others.

Father, help us to provide the cool waters of friendship and the shadows of understanding as we face life's problems.

AUGUST 17. *Fear not, for I am with thee, and will bless thee.*—GENESIS 26:24

Often a phrase from a longer passage comes to have special meaning to individuals. These eleven words cover a multitude of situations. There is no law which says that such sections cannot be used as personal mottoes when special help is needed, although clarity is added when entire long passages can be read in full context. Whatever the problems of this particular month, there is strength in remembering that God is present and that no fear needs to gain the upper hand.

Father, when we are fearful for ourselves or others, give us the inner assurance that thou art here to bless with faith.

AUGUST 18. *But I have called you friends.*—JOHN
15:15

When the family moved to a new neighborhood, the
children got acquainted first, and the mother was lonely
for her old friends. Then a letter arrived from a former
neighbor, saying, "I am so glad for those who will find in
you a new friend as soon as you begin to get acquainted."
Thus given confidence, the newcomer began to wave at
those nearest and soon began to collect new friends. Any
day is a day to find a new friend.

Eternal Friend, fill our hearts with friendly thoughts of
others, that together we may serve thee better.

AUGUST 19. *But I will settle him in mine house and
in my kingdom for ever: and his throne shall be established for evermore.*—I CHRONICLES 17:14

That word "settle" applies to so many things, including
settling into a new house. This is a frequent summer
occupation, with new locations chosen while the children
are out of school. It is important also to "settle" the mind
and heart, determining to be cheerful in such a move, or
to hold to the ideals of the father while he is away on
business or military service. All decisions are easier when
God is enthroned in the heart as King.

Father, help us to settle it now, once and for all, that we will always honor thee as King of our lives.

AUGUST 20. *Come ye yourselves apart into a desert place, and rest a while.*—MARK 6:31

As she watered the flower box by her window, the friend said, "This is my personal desert island." She kept the box abloom with bright red petunias in hottest summer days, and covered over with low growing rose geraniums through the other blooming months of the year. As she surveyed their bright loveliness and poured water from the green plastic sprinkling can, she let her mind rest from routine and turned her heart from problems. Her place of rest was small but effective.

Father, help us to clear a little "desert place" of aloneness in our busy lives, so that we may rest and commune with thee.

AUGUST 21. *Thanks be unto God for his unspeakable gift.*—II CORINTHIANS 9:15

Splashing water over their red and blue bathing suits, the youngest children played happily in the wading pool. Beyond the wall leading into the deeper water, the older children practiced their diving technique. Watching this happy activity, their mother looked up from her knitting and said to a friend: "I have forgotten to send a check to the camp for handicapped children. I'm going to do it today out of gratitude that my family is having such a wonderful day together."

Father, as we enjoy our lavish blessings of health, may we remember to include others in our personal financial planning.

AUGUST 22. *And he shall be like a tree planted by the rivers of water, that bringeth forth his fruit in his season.*—PSALM 1:3

One of the rich joys of the summer is to return to a favorite park or the old home and find that the trees have grown larger, with even more green leafy shade to make silhouetted patterns on the lawn beneath. The gracious beauty of an old tree is a blessing on an August day. The scripture says that the godly man or woman shall take on these characteristics. In the leisure of a hot summer day beneath a tree there is time for meditation on the beauty of growth toward God.

Father, we do want to be more godly in our lives, and to grow more lovely because our roots are grounded in thee.

AUGUST 23. *For there stood by me this night the angle of God, whose I am, and whom I serve.*—ACTS 27:23

Sometimes there are fears in trying new modes of conveyance, whether this be a first flight by air, or a trip by muleback high into the rugged mountain country. Some parents find they must fight worry and sleepless nights when the children are out late on vacation jaunts with the family automobile. In an age which has become skeptical of "angels," it is well to revive occasionally the memory of Paul's trust in the angels of God and their protection, which brought the ship safely to shore.

Father, return us safely from vacation journeys that we may be refreshed to do thy will in our daily activities.

AUGUST 24. *Be not overcome of evil, but overcome evil with good.*—ROMANS 12:21

As blue haze settles over the landscape at twilight on the hottest days of August, there is often a feeling that evil is likewise spreading over the world. This belief is reinforced by the news that comes over radio and television, often intruding into a summer vacation hideaway so that the family resolves to leave such instruments behind on future opportunities for rest. When such depression penetrates the heart, it is time to resolve anew to accept the Bible counsel: "Overcome evil with good."

God, we feel defeated as we see how much needs to be accomplished, and we ask thee to help us use our talents for good.

AUGUST 25. *Go to the ant, thou sluggard; consider her ways, and be wise.*—PROVERBS 6:6

An interesting pastime on a lazy summer day is to watch ants scurrying in and out of their hole in the sand, beneath the shade tree in the yard. Little by little they bring up enough portions of sand so that a hill surrounds their habitation. Their constant busyness has been the fact most often commented upon by those who would emulate them, but it is also true that they have a wonderfully organized system of cooperation. Summer is the time to make plans for group action of family and clubs.

Father, as we rest in summer vacations help us to build into our hearts the wish and willingness to work well with others.

AUGUST 26. *And he shall be thy spokesman unto the people.*—EXODUS 4:16

A popular form of summer entertainment used to be the annual chautauqua. Now a highpoint of many vacations is attendance at some out-door amphitheater which presents musical artists of high calibre, or historical pageants based on legends of the area. There is a universal need for a "spokesman," and summer is a good time to listen, and to read the Bible's words of wisdom.

God, we are glad that thou hast left us "spokesmen" in the pages of the Bible, that we may hear anew from thee.

AUGUST 27. *He being not a forgetful hearer, but a doer of the work, this man shall be blessed in his deed.* —JAMES 1:25

How many plans are made at the beginning of this month, but not carried out because of heat or just plain laziness. Perhaps this was the summer that the intent was to finish some clothes for the nearby orphanage, or to clean out the bookcases to see which books could be spared for the church library. Maybe promises have been made definitely to committee chairmen to turn in the clothes or the books, and now the summer is nearly over without the tasks accomplished. Blessing lies in taking action.

Father, help us to redeem the time, taking personal initiative to meet our commitments of sharing.

AUGUST 28. *Ye are the light of the world. A city that is set on an hill cannot be hid.*—MATTHEW 5:14

A memorable moment of any vacation is the first glimpse of a fabled city of beauty, particularly if that area can be seen in the distance, with lights flickering in welcome. It is only necessary to close the eyes long afterward to recall every detail of such a beautiful experience in travel. We forget that each day we take a journey, and that others look to us expecting to find light and radiance, as the city on the hill.

Lord of light, give us a new loveliness as we carry our lamps along the road we travel together.

AUGUST 29. *Jesus said unto him, If thou canst believe, all things are possible to him that believeth.* —MARK 9:23

Little by little each day becomes shorter, and all of a sudden it seems that the last full month of summer is nearly over, with fall straight ahead. Then it is that a young person who may have seemed to idle away all the hot months will see that he does need more education if he is to prepare for the kind of job he really wants. It is never too late to make such a decision. Faith to believe in what can be accomplished by application is the first step toward success.

159

Father, we are glad that thou dost ever hold before us the possibility of accomplishment through belief in thee.

AUGUST 30. *I am a stranger in the earth: hide not thy commandments from me.*—PSALM 119:19

As summer's familiar patterns break up into new forms of routine, there is sometimes a momentary feeling of strangeness. Heartstrings are stretched to the breaking point as children leave home for the first time, either for school or to go to another city to work, or into military service. All of us at times feel we are strangers, here on the earth, and it is then that we need to remember again that we do have a guidebook, good for all generations, in the Bible's commandments.

God, help us to take the commandments with us, wherever life leads us as this summer goes into the calendar of years.

AUGUST 31. *He that gathereth in summer is a wise son.*—PROVERBS 10:5

So many wonderful memories fill the years as the result of simple summer pleasures—the picnic in the park, a hike in the mountains, the finding of a special shell at the sandy beach. All these speak of fellowship with nature, and often with loved ones and friends including new acquaintances. The blessings of summer can be gathered together in the heart as a reservoir of energy for fresh and joyous pursuits in the fall.

Father, for the happy accumulation of days of the summer, accept our thanks, and go with us into fall activities.

September

HEAVENLY FATHER, THERE ARE SO
MANY LESSONS WE MUST LEARN.
KEEP US HUMBLE PUPILS IN THE
SCHOOL OF LIFE, EVER REACHING OUT
TO HELP OUR FELLOW SEEKERS AFTER
TRUTH.

SEPTEMBER 1. *So he fed them according to the integrity of his heart; and guided them by the skilfulness of his hands.*—PSALM 78:72

School days and books automatically come to mind when brisk September strides into the year. One of the purposes of all true learning is to acquire integrity of personality, and the ability to use the hands in service for self and others. This is easier when the individual is relying on the God who gives life and knowledge, and who is a loving teacher in the earthly school of experience.

Father, we thank thee for giving each of us a birthday in thy great and eternal Book of Life.

SEPTEMBER 2. *And Saul also went home to Gibeah; and there went with him a band of men, whose hearts God had touched.*—I SAMUEL 10:26

Early in September occurs the American holiday of Labor Day, which provides an extra day to go home to visit relatives, or return from a summer camping experience, or perhaps just keep busy at home tasks, preparing for new school experiences. How wonderful it is when this weekend shows that the individual is surrounded by a band of relatives and friends whose hearts have been touched by God, so that there is rich fellowship at home, school, or play.

God, we are grateful for the band of friends and loved ones who have touched our hearts and brought us closer to thee.

SEPTEMBER 3. *And he rose up, and passed over the river, and set his face toward the mount Gilead.*—GENESIS 31:21

At the time of beginning again as summer ends, it becomes necessary to make decisions and to rise up and sometimes cross over the river of traditional paths, setting the heart and mind toward new hills of hope. Young people find that they must call upon fresh resources of courage when the moment comes to leave for school or military service. Older loved ones, more skilled in hiding emotion, feel their lips trembling. Life is a constant facing toward the mountains of achievement.

God, be with us in our climb toward the ever-beckoning hills of experience that there may be joy in the daily journey.

SEPTEMBER 4. *For by thee I have run through a troop: by my God have I leaped over a wall.*—II Samuel 22:30

Wistfully the friend confessed, "I thought I was making progress, but I seem to have run into a stone wall." Like many she thought that the way through was to chisel painfully, stone by stone. Others seem to think it is necessary to try to find a place for faltering feet to climb to the top, despite perilous falls backward. The Bible testimony is that God can give grace and endurance so that it becomes possible to stop crawling, and instead to leap over the obstructing walls of life. Faith gives the needed impetus.

Lord, grant us every ounce of energy which we need to meet our commitments at home and business in behalf of thee.

SEPTEMBER 5. *Look unto the heavens, and see; and behold the clouds which are higher than thou.*—JOB 35:5

One of the joys of a weekend away from home or a day spent in the yard is the opportunity to look up at the sky and see how high are the clouds from the earth. It is natural to forget the size of God's immensity when we are involved in routine tasks. Sometimes this very vastness makes us feel frightened when we undertake some large enterprise, such as entering graduate school or moving to a new location. In such moments it is wonderful to recall that the God of the immense universe is the same God who cares for his children.

God, may we never forget to look up to the clouds to find new strength when we become immersed in pettiness.

SEPTEMBER 6. *And said unto me, Thou art my servant O Israel, in whom I will be glorified.*—ISAIAH 49:3

Writing home from his military service, a fine young man told his parents that he had decided to return to school when his tour of duty was ended. Before he left, he had been tired of school books, but now he saw clearly what it was he wanted to do in the way of service to others. It was a wonderful moment for all the family, as are all such instances of decision. When even a simple decision for good is made it becomes possible for God to glorify daily study and actions to benefit others.

Father, in this season of decisions help us to make the right choices for service in clubs, churches, and community projects.

SEPTEMBER 7. *These things have I spoken unto you, that my joy might remain in you, and that your joy might be full.*—JOHN 15:11

Advice is given freely in this particular month, as children enter school for the first time or begin new jobs in distant cities. It is natural to rebel against some of the axioms which families impart, but in later years the advice may be seen to have led to right action because it was so deeply imbedded in the mind through repetition. Loving advice has at its heart the wish to increase the joys of living.

Father, keep us from being rebellious at the words of counsel from loved ones, and help us to use what is best for us.

SEPTEMBER 8. *Now he was ruddy, and withal of a beautiful countenance, and goodly to look to.*—I SAMUEL 16:12

Freshly scrubbed faces and slicked down hair of little boys with suntanned legs and arms from a summer in the open air, greet the elementary school teachers when school begins. The young woman far away from home for the first time at college may be attracted by the handsome lad in her early morning class. There is pleasure in manliness which is "goodly," and this can be cultivated through clean thinking and generous kindly action.

Father, may we strive to be goodly in our appearance and actions, knowing how closely this word is allied to "godly."

SEPTEMBER 9. *Let us lift up our heart with our hands unto God in the heavens.*—LAMENTATIONS 3:41

Schoolteachers facing girls in plaid gingham dresses and boys with bright shirts can tell fairly soon who will be the children to make the most progress. An experienced principal tells parents that the boys and girls who really want to learn will accomplish much, even if their native intelligence is a little less than others who do not choose to work. The problem of true education becomes that of making heart and hand work together for maximum growth of personality.

God, there is so much we need to learn, but here we offer hearts and hands for the projects of thy kingdom.

SEPTEMBER 10. *The sacrifices of God are a broken spirit: a broken and a contrite heart, O God, thou wilt not despise.*—PSALM 51:17

When the bills for a school day wardrobe come into the home, or it becomes necessary to send a new check for tuition, sacrifice is very apparent in many family budgets. One of the real sources of discontent in the modern age is the selfish wish to own more in the face of mounting expenses. Often there are quarrels as to which projects are the most deserving. Sacrifice calls for breaking the spirit of selfishness, and the contrite wish to make the maximum use of the many blessings which God has given freely.

God, keep our hearts right within us that the expenditure of funds may be done with integrity and uprightness.

SEPTEMBER 11. *So the posts went with the letters from the king and his princes throughout all Israel and Judah.*—II CHRONICLES 30:6

Ceremony has always attached to the arrival of the mail, from the earliest days of the kings. Steamships carry special flags when they are bringing mail into port. In some places the postal carriers, walking the village streets or riding their motorized carts, wear an identifying uniform. As September events swing into action, it is time to get out the stationery and write that first letter to a child at school, or remember the boy from the church who is serving his country overseas.

Father, forgive us our neglect of family and friends, because we do not sit down to write the comforting note of encouragement.

SEPTEMBER 12. *And he shall be unto thee a restorer of thy life, and a nourisher of thine old age.*—RUTH 4:15

Fall months bring many changes in family routines. Sometimes this means bringing into the home an elderly relative unable to provide longer for himself in familiar quarters. When this happens the verse for today, which refers to the Lord and his goodness, can be of great practical help to all ages of the family. One who relies on God for help in all circumstances can adjust better to changing days.

God, keep us from being rigidly right and refusing to accept the realities which may become necessary as the years mount.

SEPTEMBER 13. *And now, behold, I go bound in the spirit unto Jerusalem, not knowing the things that shall befall me there.*—ACTS 20:22

A popular feature of most morning newspapers is the little column on astrology. A surprising number who claim they are not superstitious still like to read and comment upon this, sometimes in a lighthearted detached way. There is in each of us the wish to know what lies ahead, and it takes real courage to move forward when the way seems especially dark and unknown. We have the example from the Bible of great people who walked with God, even though their spirits felt bound and not free.

Father, often we feel a heaviness in our hearts at signs of change, and we ask for courage to meet the modern demands.

SEPTEMBER 14. *Let your conversation be without covetousness; and be content with such things as ye have.*—HEBREWS 13:5

Announcement of the club's first fall program said that it would consist of reports of summer vacations. One member who had met with health problems and financial reverses confided to a friend that she did not really want to attend. Fortunately her friend was able to persuade her to forget personal disappointments and rejoice with others.

Thus her own zest for living was restored, and she became aware of her own blessings.

God, when we deny ourselves pleasures because of envy of others, grant us clearer vision to enjoy that which we do have.

SEPTEMBER 15. *And let the beauty of the Lord our God be upon us.*—PSALM 90:17

As September's blue haze lifts, exposing the world to bright fall sunshine, it is possible to get a fresh perspective of beauty. The golden sun is reflected in the first blossoming goldenrod along the roadside, and contrasts with the wild purple asters, offering their abundant beauty in the grass. Each season brings its own precious gifts of loveliness and shows the care of God for the world and those who live therein. Yet only those who pause to look can receive God's beauty.

God, we would indeed let thy beauty come into our hearts this day, that we may grow in grace and loveliness.

SEPTEMBER 16. *Remember the former things of old: for I am God, and there is none else; I am God, and there is none like me.*—ISAIAH 46:9

Remembering routine is one of the tasks which faces all ages around the middle of each September. The child going into first grade has to remember what it was like in kindergarten, only now he is older and sits in a larger desk. Even after a summer's lapse it is necessary to remember details of keeping accurate attendance records at Sunday school. When such remembering involves thinking how God has blessed the past, the future has within it many abundant blessings.

Father, let us remember thee in our past experiences so that we may understand thee more fully in days ahead.

SEPTEMBER 17. *And whosoever shall compel thee to go a mile, go with him twain.*—MATTHEW 5:41

On her first day at the new college campus, the freshman met a white-haired man hurrying up the walk. Timidly she asked him the way to the school library. Instantly he turned around and walked with her, asking en route about her home and family. Not until the opening convocation did she learn that this kindness had been shown by the busy president of the institution. His example helped her develop a sense of personal responsibility in accepting school and alumnae assignments.

Father, take away from us any feeling of being compelled to help, but let us accept opportunities graciously.

SEPTEMBER 18. *And they did all eat, and were filled.*—MARK 6:42

Stocking the food shelves after the informal meals of summer is a problem encountered in many homes. Some people make it a habit to place their canned goods in rotating order, so that it is easy to reach up in a hurry and find a can of beans, tomatoes, or corn when preparing dinner for the family. Women's perennial involvement with food is a normal part of the routine of fall, and there is great satisfaction when all have been fed. Many are the hungers of the heart which also should be considered, and plans must be made for meeting these needs.

Father, we are hungry for the spiritual food which will satisfy our desires and strengthen us for today's tasks.

SEPTEMBER 19. *And be clothed with humility: for God resisteth the proud, and giveth grace to the humble.*—I PETER 5:5

Getting clothing in shape for fall is an inevitable chore of September. My, how the children have grown, the mother discovers as she surveys how short is the dress which was long in spring before the days spent out of doors. Or it may be that an adult's dress needs to be shortened, having stretched out of shape on the hangers over the months. These outer garments may go out of fashion, but the heart's best clothing never changes, for it is graced with humility and moves quietly among the proud.

God, give us humble hearts to accept thy great goodness to us, and to use all blessings to thy honor and glory.

SEPTEMBER 20. *And a certain woman named Martha received him into her home.*—LUKE 10:38

Hospitality and September go hand in hand. This is often the time when arrangements are made for "boarding out" for a special year of study, or living for a while in a new locale. Firm are the friendships forged in such foster homes by adults who share the same interests. And it may prove an actual lifesaver to children who have been abandoned by delinquent parents, or to babies put out for adoption when other homes open their arms in loving welcome. Such actions reflect the heart which is open to share with others.

God, there are little ways in which we may open our homes more widely to others. Help us to do this today.

SEPTEMBER 21. *Come unto me, all ye that labour and are heavy laden, and I will give you rest.*—MATTHEW 11:28

Administrative tasks of getting a new year organized, or the house in order for company can result in deep fatigue. Looking ahead to the many months before the routine can change brings added tiredness, until a man may say, "I guess I was just born tired." Such moments of depression can be kept at a minimum if a plan is set up to try to rest from labors by refreshing the mind through positive thinking of surrounding blessings. The Bible promises rest through God.

Father, give to us the blessings of restoration from labor as we seek a proper balance of our strength and duties.

SEPTEMBER 22. *And the court was full of the brightness of the Lord's glory.*—EZEKIEL 10:4

A brilliant day of early fall, with a breeze bearing its hint of colder days to come, can fill the heart with enthusiasm for starting new tasks. Even a glance out the window toward the border of bronze chrysanthemums reminds us of the glorious days ahead and gives new energy. If this can be combined with the efforts of others interested in the same projects, much can be accomplished for community and church, so that the Lord's glory is shown forth.

Father, help us to keep bright the trusts committed to us, that thy glory may be seen clearly even by those who scoff.

SEPTEMBER 23. *And carry down the man a present, a little balm, and a little honey, spices, and myrrh, nuts, and almonds.*—GENESIS 43:11

That moment when a package from home is placed in the hands of a son or daughter serving in military service or away at school is a high point of the day. All of us love to receive presents, even if it is just an advertising gimmick which we know to be from a firm hoping for our business. In such there is "a little balm" for the lonely, an attitude of personal recognition which builds happy associations. This is a technique which all may learn to add to daily happiness.

Father, we are glad for the joy of simple presents, and we want to retain a childlike interest in all gifts of love.

SEPTEMBER 24. *Now the things which I write unto you, behold, before God, I lie not.*—GALATIANS 1:20

To be certain of facts is one of the best feelings a student can have when taking an examination. Later in a job it may take what reporters call "leg work" to uncover the exact situation at city hall, or find the correct spelling of the names of the committee members working for the new park. If such information must be correct in school or the business world, how much more important is it for the heart to be sure of its spiritual truths which can be tested through experience.

God, keep our lives from being lies, but may they reflect the truth which we have learned through prayer and tested daily.

SEPTEMBER 25. *And Jesus said unto them, I am the bread of life: he that cometh to me shall never hunger; and he that believeth on me shall never thirst.* —JOHN 6:35

Standing before the jury, the lawyer summed up the case in a few words. The housewives and businessmen were able to understand the situation because of his clear explanation. Therefore they knew what action to take. Fortunately many Bible verses are complete in themselves, summarizing faith and action. All God's creatures know hunger and thirst, in whatever land or circumstance. Realistically this search is recognized as the Bible outlines action for personal peace.

Father, as we go about our tasks of preparing food for loved ones, let us be concerned also for their spiritual sustenance.

SEPTEMBER 26. *My doctrine shall drop as the rain, my speech shall distil as the dew, as the small rain upon the tender herb, and as the showers upon the grass.* —DEUTERONOMY 32:2

New theologians present new doctrines. Often the freshman entering a class in religion will begin to question his own beliefs and those of his family. It is a comfort to know, as the Bible promises, that God's true doctrine shall be as beneficial as the rain causing the fragrant herbs to grow. Like showers of September, bringing cool waters to the dusty earth, the true doctrine of God refreshes the heart.

God, we want to be true to all that is best, and not be confused by the clamor of voices and sounds of uncertainty.

SEPTEMBER 27. *And now, behold, we are in thine hand: as it seemeth good and right unto thee to do unto us, do.*—JOSHUA 9:25

Perfect trust in the powers that be is hard to come by in this age, whether in a college, a school club, or the administration of a church. In a democracy concern for leadership is rightly held by the individual as his own prerogative. In matters of the soul the situation is very different. Complete allegiance to God is demanded as he is revealed to us daily through our prayer and meditation as we ask for help in specific situations.

God, forgive us for our failure to trust thee, and keep us willing to do what thou wouldst have us do for thee.

SEPTEMBER 28. *When I lie down, I say, When shall I arise, and the night be gone? and I am full of tossings to and fro unto the dawning of the day.*—JOB 7:4

Sometimes muggy September weather seems like a wet blanket making it difficult to sleep. Such nights complicate the normal problems of family living and special worries about school or business. Light sleepers find themselves prowling the house in search of a cookie or an apple. Another device is to go to the window and look up at the stars, glittering bright in the early autumnal sky. Their serene beauty reminds one of God's eternal care and the opportunities ahead when the fresh day dawns.

Father, still our restless tossing to and fro with the sure knowledge of thy unfailing care and concern for us.

SEPTEMBER 29. *Now the just shall live by faith: but if any man draw back, my soul shall have no pleasure in him.*—HEBREWS 10:38

No month passes without its testing of faith, through the death of a loved one or the remembrance of happy things past which are changed by sad new situations. If trouble comes abruptly it is usually harder to face than when it is of long duration. All testing situations call for faith and the moving forward to the solution of the

179

problem. Once committed we must keep on, even when tempted to turn back on the road of faith.

Father, let thy love shine clearly through today's circumstances, so that we may walk by faith on the prescribed pathway.

SEPTEMBER 30. *Boast not thyself of tomorrow; for thou knowest not what a day may bring forth.*—PROVERBS 27:1

As September experiences merge with the past, it is natural to think of what needs to be accomplished in the month ahead. Yet the Bible frequently points out that time should be broken down into days, and that we do not know what even this small segment of time may bring of joy or sorrow. This much we do know, that we can turn the month which is leaving into God's hands and trust him for whatever lies ahead.

Father, the month has brought different experiences to each of us, but we are alike in our need to learn more of thee.

October

GOD OF FRESH BEGINNINGS, GRANT US
NEW IMPETUS TO SERVE THEE. MAY
OUR LIVES BE CHANGED BY COMPAS-
SIONATE SERVICE EVEN AS THE TREES
TAKE ON THEIR GLORIOUS AUTUMN
COLORINGS.

OCTOBER 1. *Up; for this is the day.*—Judges 4:14

October is the "getting up month" a friend remarked
as she got out of her chair to answer the telephone
announcing another committee meeting. It almost seems
to be a time when the year begins all over again, as
fall schedules launch fresh activities, encouraged by the
cool autumnal breezes. There is joy in seizing the present
moment, and knowing this is the day for happy action.

Father, forgive us for not making the most of each day,
and help us use today's gift of time in unselfish service.

OCTOBER 2. *For the Lord shall greatly bless thee in the land which the Lord thy God giveth thee for an inheritance to possess it.*—DEUTERONOMY 15:4

With the landscape so beautiful at harvest time, there is a swelling of pride in the heart of the person who looks upon the area where he makes his home. This inheritance may be forgotten in hot days of summer, or the storms of winter, but it cannot be overlooked with the golden haze of October adding a special lustrous halo to the trees, flowers, and shrubs. All this natural beauty of October can lead the heart to God.

Father, we are grateful that thou dost provide daily beauty as manna to bless our regular paths and feed our hearts.

OCTOBER 3. *When I call to remembrance the unfeigned faith that is in thee, which dwelt first in thy grandmother. . .* —II TIMOTHY 1:5

When the fields turn ripe with harvest, the mind often has nostalgic thoughts of the pioneers who first reclaimed the land which now produces in such abundance. Many were the women who worked beside their men in the fields, clearing the trees and stumps so that the seed corn and wheat could go into the ground. They were also the pioneers who sowed the spiritual seeds of thrift, prudence, and industry, and above all honored God with their faith.

Such a rich inheritance is a current blessing whenever it is continued in good works.

God, we are grateful for the pioneers who planted the harvest of blessing we reap today and which we would cherish.

OCTOBER 4. *Her ways are ways of pleasantness, and all her paths are peace.*—PROVERBS 3:17

Although this verse refers to the word "wisdom" it seems especially adapted to the special knowledge that is inherent in the nature of October. For looking at the ripened fields bordered with their tall sunflowers which the swift flying birds seem to mistake for trees, one has in the heart a feeling of peace and tranquility. Such moments are to be cherished and added to the year's pleasant memories.

God, we ask for the special wisdom which comes by cultivating peaceful moments with thee and enjoying thy pleasant pastures.

OCTOBER 5. *And they shall be mine, saith the Lord of hosts, in that day when I make up my jewels.*—MAL-ACHI 3:17

Sparkling red, yellow, and orange jewels swing from the leafy trees in the orchards of October, as the moment comes for the harvesting of apples and plums. In various latitudes the time pattern may be different, but the beautiful shading of the growing jewels is essentially the same, as the fruit ripens into splendid colors, showing it is ready to take to the home table. Likewise, each of us is a living jewel, growing in the garden of God until the day of harvest and the time of entering the eternal homeland.

God, we are grateful that we may grow, each in our own way, as colorful jewels awaiting the final harvest.

OCTOBER 6. *Every man according as he purposeth in his heart, so let him give; not grudgingly, or of necessity: for God loveth a cheerful giver.*—II CORINTHIANS 9:7

Lavishly October bestows its gifts of a bountiful harvest on the world in the wealth of golden chrysanthemums and the showers of leaves, falling like coins to the ground. And this is the time usually when the annual drives for funds begin in communities, whether large or small. Those who ask for the contributions often meet with "static" from people asked to contribute, and it is hard to keep a happy equilibrium in door to door canvassing. Remembering God's bounty as seen in natural beauty can help to open purses more generously.

Father, help us pay our rent on this beautiful earth by helping others who need the services of community and church agencies.

OCTOBER 7. *And the water ran round about the altar; and he filled the trench also with water.*—I KINGS 18:35

If warm weather continues into fall, the problem of watering the garden to keep it moist after the drying winds becomes one of importance to the family. Water figures in many of the ceremonies of Bible times, and it is frequently used as a symbol for living. Water can be interpreted also as the financial substance which keeps philanthropic organizations in good shape. The Bible reminds us that even the altar was surrounded with water, an example of abundance for givers today.

Father, we want the water of life to flow abundantly through our own personalities, so help us to keep open the channels.

OCTOBER 8. *And the feast of harvest, the firstfruits of thy labours, which thou hast sown in the field . . .* —EXODUS 23:16

Even this fragment of verse points the mind toward that happy occasion, "the feast of harvest," still carried out in many churches. Sometimes young people take charge, setting up booths in which may be displayed the brilliant orange pumpkin, the ripened clusters of purple grapes, the shocks of yellow corn. If the firstfruits of labors are shared and enjoyed the hard work is forgotten, and harvest becomes a time of happiness. So it should be with the work of disciplining the heart so sins are weeded out, and there is a harvest of contentment.

Father, we would return to thee that which is best, in deep gratitude for thy daily care of the fields of our lives.

OCTOBER 9. *So built we the wall; and all the wall was joined together unto the half thereof: for the people had a mind to work.*—NEHEMIAH 4:6

Getting together in this month of beginning again to work on group projects makes for sociability and accomplishes much. Whether this involves striping the church parking lot so fenders do not get smashed on Sunday mornings, or a meeting of the women to plan for a holiday bazaar, the one essential ingredient is "a mind to work." This is what is needed also if the individual is to begin a long deferred hobby or night school project, for it provides motivation.

Father, grant us a mind to work at our own particular tasks, thus contributing our best to the common good.

OCTOBER 10. *And he that sat upon the throne said, Behold, I make all things new.*—REVELATION 21:5

In a moment of fatigue, a friend confessed, "I really dread for this month of October to get into full swing, for it means that all the same old committees and meetings begin again, and that there are the same dues and special funds." By her words and attitude she was showing how much she needed to get a fresh point of view, so that the old projects could be enjoyed with new zest. A spirit of unselfish service can give new impetus to familiar projects needing funds.

Father, we bring old problems of money and organizations to thee, and ask for wisdom to try a new effective approach.

OCTOBER 11. *Though thy beginning was small, yet thy latter end should greatly increase.*—JOB 8:7

Even a tiny idea begun in fall can lead to great enjoyment before the year's end. A club sponsor expressed it this way, "You can accomplish anything, if you just begin soon enough." She said this the day she purchased white burlap to begin making two dozen miniature angels to give to her "girls" at the holiday season. Fall's reviving energy through cooler weather can be turned to good use in beginning an afghan to keep warm the legs of an

187

elderly friend in a rest home, or painting toys for an orphanage.

God, with our limited funds and small talents, help us to grow from tiny beginnings to increased influence for good.

OCTOBER 12. *And when it was day, they knew not the land: but they discovered a certain creek with a shore, into the which they were minded, if it were possible, to thrust in the ship.*—ACTS 27:39

On this day, anniversary of the discovery of America, there are many reminders of others who have discovered safety after long journeys. Even as the early disciples went on a voyage of discovery in the early missionary journeys, that adventure is available to each of us today. For there is no discovery quite like that of finding new facets of personality, greater heights of friendship, deepening affection for loved ones.

God, even as we discover new things about ourselves, make our lives continuing adventures of discovery of thy love.

OCTOBER 13. *And the Lord God planted a garden eastward in Eden; and there he put the man whom he had formed.*—GENESIS 2:8

One of the joys of the month of October is the opportunity to plant bulbs which will blossom in the springtime. The moment comes when, with trowel in hand, one digs the hole to receive the daffodil bulb. How scaly are the brown layers of natural wrappings, which one by one will slip away as the bulb dreams in the soil through the winter months. Then some morning will appear the green stalk, and the golden blossom will soon follow—a symbol of God's affection for mankind placed in his earthly kingdom.

God, for gardens accept our thanks, and help us prepare our hearts also for receiving the blossoms of blessings.

OCTOBER 14. *Do ye look on things after the outward appearance?*—II CORINTHIANS 10:7

This searching question helps a man define himself as he gives answer. The person who does look on the outward appearance is frequently disappointed when he tries to go deeper into a relationship and discovers one who is all for outer show. Whereas in the harvest season it is easy to see that what seems a miserable small seed with no possibility of growth may produce large vegetables to fill the larder to overflowing. Judgment should be reserved until outward and inner appearance balance.

189

God, forgive us our flighty responses that do not wait for normal growth to reveal the true stature of our acquaintances.

OCTOBER 15. *And this I pray, that your love may abound yet more and more.*—PHILIPPIANS 1:9

Family gatherings in the month of fruitful harvests have special significance of beautiful fellowship when based on mutual love and respect. These are virtues which grow slowly through the years, and glow with a special halo when experiences of sorrow and defeat have been surmounted in the passage of the years together. A harvest of loving fellowship from one family circle can prove a blessing to all within a church or community. It is an ideal worth striving for in any home circle.

Father, bless all who are in position to reap a harvest of love, and help us to cultivate kindness and compassion.

OCTOBER 16. *So we thy people and sheep of thy pasture will give thee thanks for ever: we will shew forth thy praise to all generations.*—PSALM 79:13

As fall shadows lengthen, bringing shorter days, it is good to see the sheep in the pasture grazing on what is left of the year's crops. Sometimes the cattle must come into the barns to be fed from purchased grain because the storms arrive early. How wonderful it is when the heart has come to accept the fact that truly there is a spiritual pasture land available in the average year, even in stormy emotional cycles.

Father, we are indeed the sheep of thy eternal pasture, and we are glad that thou dost meet our every need when we ask.

OCTOBER 17. *But let every man prove his own work, and then he shall have rejoicing in himself alone, and not in another.*—GALATIANS 6:4

Harvest time in the fields is a time for examination, and determining whether the seed corn fulfilled the expectations announced by the catalogues. It is the occasion for the housewife to admire the new white cascading chrysanthemum she plans to use in decorating the church for a wedding. The Bible encourages each of us to examine ourselves to see how the spiritual harvest is progressing in our own hearts, without casting envious glances at another's victories.

God, let us not overlook the necessity to tend to the harvest of our own minds and hearts as we grow in thy kingdom.

OCTOBER 18. *For as touching the ministering to the saints, it is superfluous for me to write to you.*—II CORINTHIANS 9:1

Speaking of a gracious woman of the community a leader said, "She always knows the right thing to do, and does it." It is truly "superfluous" to give advice to such a person as to how to treat those in need of hospitality. Most of us stand in need of correction from time to time, and all our mistakes are based on the inability to place ourselves in the other person's position. Happy is the heart which sees the situation through eyes of gracious understanding.

Father, we would not forget to minister to the saints who live modestly near us, bearing their own burdens with dignity.

OCTOBER 19. *For here have we no continuing city, but we seek one to come.*—HEBREWS 13:14

A mood of restlessness is part of the prevailing power of October, when the haze of Indian summer sweeps over the land. Perhaps this refers to some primitive time in the history of mankind when the coming of autumn meant that individuals must cease their migrating and find a place of safety for the winter. When we are restless it is a part of our common humanity, for together we seek an eternal city.

God, help us to subdue our restless spirits, turning energy toward projects for good in our transient stay on earth.

OCTOBER 20. *Rooted and built up in him, and established in the faith, as ye have been taught, abounding therein with thanksgiving.*—COLOSSIANS 2:7

Roots grow deep, as laborers discover when moving out orchards to make way for a modern subdivision. Sometimes equipment must dig deep into the soil and then extend widely in several directions to get all the side roots. Seeing such a kingly monarch of a tree lying on its side by the road reminds us of the importance of putting down such roots for the living years. The soul which is rooted in God also stands firm despite onslaughts of circumstances until the appointed end.

God, let our roots grow a little deeper in the soil of faith, that we may stand erect against the skyline of events.

OCTOBER 21. *Though thou shouldest make thy nest as high as the eagle, I will bring thee down from thence, saith the Lord.*—JEREMIAH 49:16

Wide wings soaring on the autumn winds, the large birds fly overhead. Sometimes there are seagulls returning inland for the colder months, or wild ducks flying south to escape winter storms. Even the proud eagle may be seen occasionally in the far reaches of the west, soaring toward its nest high in the hills. Often we long to soar like the birds, and to build a nest away from civilization, but since Old Testament times it has been the plan of God to keep us humble and happy servants.

Father, when we are tempted to flee, like the birds, to easier, more favorable climates, help us to keep to thy chosen ways.

OCTOBER 22. *The good man is perished out of the earth: . . . they hunt every man his brother with a net.* —MICAH 7:2

Generation after generation, winds of war sweep over the land even as the breezes of autumn stir the fields. The Bible often speaks for modern mankind in telling of the way in which man hunts his brother, even as men go into the field with guns for the wild prey when the hunting seasons are open. It is hard to keep cheerful in the face of such continued inhumanity, but the Bible promises the ultimate victory of good.

God, we feel hunted by the evil of our times, as though we would be snared, and we need thy help in escaping temptation.

194

OCTOBER 23. *And the shapes of the locusts were like unto horses prepared unto battle.*—REVELATION 9:7

As brown leaves fall to the ground they make interesting patterns and cause barren spots on the limbs which assume grotesque shapes in the twilight moments of an autumn day. Depending upon the predominant mood of the mind, the shapes become fearful or friendly. When a dread emotion has taken hold of the body it is easy to think of a tiny locust as a large animal prepared for battle. One of the tasks of modern living is to keep the dragons of machines from assuming too large shapes and sizes.

God, keep our vision focused on thee, that we may see details aright and live our lives in proper proportions of service.

OCTOBER 24. *It was planted in a good soil by great waters, that it might bring forth branches, and that it might bear fruit, that it might be a goodly vine.*—EZEKIEL 17:8

Vineyards ripe with purple grapes while the green leaves turn to red and gold form a beautiful picture framed by October. Even the fragile dust which covers the tiny grapes until they are washed in clear cold water adds to their attractive appearance. Good soil and moisture lead to branches which bear good fruit, as the month testifies.

So it is when a soul is planted in the kingdom of God to receive the water of life, bearing fruit in good deeds.

God, may our actions add to the beauty of thy world at harvest time, and not be cast aside as unworthy.

OCTOBER 25. *Make ready quickly three measures of fine meal, knead it, and make cakes upon the hearth.* —GENESIS 18:6

On a day when the October air is so clear it seems even to taste good, many women often feel impelled to do the first fall baking, looking ahead to the happiest season of the year. There is a joyous ritual in going to secure the first ripened persimmons for the making of cookies which can be mailed overseas. Perhaps this is the day to chop the nuts and raisins for the fruitcake for the family, from a recipe of cherished heritage. Such planning leads to the fellowship of sharing which blesses the family circle.

Father, for all tasks which unite us with women everywhere as we plan for our families, accept our thanks this day.

OCTOBER 26. *Therefore, my beloved brethren, be ye steadfast, unmoveable, always abounding in the work of the Lord, forasmuch as ye know that your labour is not in vain in the Lord.*—I CORINTHIANS 15:58

Working days grow crowded in October with twilight coming earlier while many tasks still remain to be accomplished. Sometimes it seems as though each fall there are even more jobs to be done at home and in community circles. Every once in a while a person must give himself a pep talk to keep in stride with the activities. The Bible foresaw this moment of need, and provided the perfect working creed in today's verse.

Lord, we give our talents anew to thee that we may not labor in vain, but be found in accustomed spots of service.

OCTOBER 27. *The effectual fervent prayer of a righteous man availeth much.*—JAMES 5:16

If the telephone rings telling of an automobile accident or the illness of a friend, there is usually a feeling of wanting to do something to help. Often it seems there is nothing tangible which can be done. Yet each of us does possess the most helpful ability of all, that of taking the matter to God in prayer. Some friends are finding that this power is multiplied when they meet together for intercessory prayer, or pause in their own homes at a specified daily hour.

197

Father, show us how to make our own prayers more effectual for others by pausing daily to listen to thy answers.

OCTOBER 28. *Their tongue is as an arrow shot out; it speaketh deceit.*—JEREMIAH 9:8

Through the woods Robin Hood and his merry men went with bows and arrows, often in search of food to last out the coming winter months. Something glamorous lingers about the bow and arrow, and many turn to it as a hobby and recreational sport. Once the arrow leaves the bow, it does not return. This is true of words spoken in deceit or anger. They cannot be called back, and often they hit their mark and maim or kill as does the arrow from the bow.

God, let us shoot the arrows of compassion from a bow which is bent with love and good intentions in behalf of others.

OCTOBER 29. *Now there are diversities of gifts, but the same Spirit.*—I CORINTHIANS 12:4

The first football game of the fall season is always an occasion for arousing school spirit. This is true among not only the current students, but many parents and townspeople, not to mention alumni who may travel from afar to share the old school ties. Such spirit is what the cheer leaders call for when the going is rough, and it is the one factor which encourages all players, whatever their places on the team. Keeping a spirit for unselfish tasks makes all of life easier, whatever our own gifts and talents may be.

Father, keep our spirits alive within us that we may quicken our energies in the tasks set before us for thee.

OCTOBER 30. *It is he that buildeth his stories in the heaven, and hath founded his troop in the earth.*— Amos 9:6

This is the time for the trooping together of children, who delight in stories of mischief and adventure. Some of these say that the very ghosts themselves walk through the earth as the time nears for All Hallow's Eve and the planning of Halloween costumes. What fun the children have in dressing up, telling ghost stories, and reading their fortunes written in lemon juice on white paper. Play is one of the blessings God planned for his troops of mankind.

God, for the joyous spirit of fun in our workaday world we are grateful and would enter in to it with active pleasure.

OCTOBER 31.   *Behold, I stand at the door, and knock:*
if any man hear my voice, and open the door, I will come
in to him, and will sup with him, and he with me.
—REVELATION 3:20

On the night when there are many knocks at the door,
the homeowner encounters small ghosts, often lisping out
"Trick or Treat." Maybe a pet has been brought along
to perform for a special sweet. Giggles and laughter
express the joy in the hearts of the children because the
door has opened to their knock. Each of us possesses the
power to keep the door shut or to answer when life
knocks at the door of our hearts. Only by opening do
we find the offered fellowship.

God, if we have kept our hearts closed to thee, help us
to open them now, that new blessings may pour into our
lives.

November

GOD, WE GIVE THEE GRATITUDE FOR
THE HALLOWED MEMORIES OF FAM-
ILY GATHERINGS IN THIS MONTH OF
THANKSGIVING. LET OUR DAILY ACTIV-
ITIES REFLECT THE HEART'S THANK-
FULNESS FOR BLESSINGS.

NOVEMBER 1. *While the earth remaineth, seedtime
and harvest, and cold and heat, and summer and winter,
and day and night shall not cease.*—GENESIS 8:22

A reminder of this precious promise from God's holy word
is visible in November when the fields are ripe for harvest
and the cold returns to many areas. Looking out on the
shocked corn, or at a plastic symbol of this in a decoration
of a city store window, one makes a momentary if silent
acknowledgment of the quick change of the seasons.

Then it is good to have the assurance of stability in change, which can be available also in personal life to those who trust God's laws.

Father, help us to so live that a harvest of good actions may result inevitably from the seeds of positive thinking.

NOVEMBER 2. *Blessed of the Lord be his land . . . and for the precious fruits brought forth by the sun, and for the precious things put forth by the moon.*—DEUTERONOMY 33:13-14

This phrase speaks of the abundance of the harvest, no matter what is native to the particular area. In orange groves, the brilliant sunshine seems reflected in the golden balls of fruit. The silvery sheen on the red-skinned apple looks like moonlight which has paused to rest on earth for a while. There is beauty in the harvest when each fruit is clearly revealed, and it will be so with the inevitable harvest of the heart.

God, help us to reflect in our daily lives the glory of the sun of righteousness and the soft loveliness of kindness.

NOVEMBER 3. *I will heal their backsliding, I will love them freely: for mine anger is turned away from him.*—HOSEA 14:4

Rich satisfaction comes in the moment of picking a beautiful red chrysanthemum from a bush which had been broken to the ground by dogs rushing through the garden. The plant which rights itself and responds to loving care often produces a beautiful blossom to grace the home in a special corner which needs brightening. There can be a similar moment of happy harvest for any heart which turns away from its broken promises and accepts the love of God freely offered to all.

Father, give us the inner satisfaction of spiritual success captured from what seemed like certain failure.

NOVEMBER 4.　*Seest thou a man that is hasty in his words? there is more hope of a fool than of him.*— PROVERBS 29:20

Often this is the month for elections, when the stature of men is clearly revealed through the words which they say or those which they leave unspoken. Many are the harsh words uttered in criticism and the deceitful ones said with promises which are not kept. It is a wonderful joy to find a man who says what he means and who means what he says. This type of integrity is a goal for any person who can control hasty words.

Father, help us to think before we speak, that we may make ourselves clearly known to others for what we represent.

NOVEMBER 5. *Whosoever hateth his brother is a murderer: and ye know that no murderer hath eternal life abiding in him.*—I JOHN 3:15

Words of hate foul the air in an election year, contrasting with the beautiful harvest in the landscape. People who would not think of using guns and bullets do not hesitate to try to tear down others with scandalous rumors, gossip, and words of hateful revenge. This stirs up the body with poisons which can lead to certain forms of illness. All such hatred is against the ideals expressed in the Bible for man's good and growth.

God, keep us from murdering our own best selves by allowing hatred to fester in our hearts for another child of thine.

NOVEMBER 6. *A friend loveth at all times.*—PROV-ERBS 17:17

Bringing an armload of pink and purple asters in from the garden, the friend said, "I love this flower, for you can use it over and over again in so many different ways." She was putting a handful into a blue vase for the kitchen, and arranging others in a nosegay to take to a friend who was ill. The flowers in their simplicity and loveliness seemed to express the love of this woman for her friends, and her concern for their welfare. Each of us can learn to enjoy beauty and our friends.

Father, if we feel friendless at times, help us to increase our love for others in all circumstances.

NOVEMBER 7. *Then Eli answered and said, Go in peace: and the God of Israel grant thee thy petition that thou hast asked of him.*—I Samuel 1:17

At the time of the beginning of fall journeys in behalf of business enterprises, church activities, or family reunions, it is wonderful to have from friends and acquaintances the happy equivalent of the beautiful phrase "Go in peace." This is what most of us want to do, day by day, whether going to a store to work or into our kitchens to cook for our families. Such peace is more possible of achievement when we continue our petitions to God in prayer, asking for virtues and guidance.

Father, give us grace to permit all we know to go in peace without interference through jealousy or possession.

NOVEMBER 8. *For where a testament is, there must also of necessity be the death of the testator.*—Hebrews 9:16

Handling the fragile white plate with the golden rim and purple violets handpainted in the center, the friend said, "This is one of the lovely dishes which came to me from the estate." She paused with a faraway look of nostalgia in her eyes, as she recalled the times she had seen this set used in another home. Because wise provision had been made for passing along tangible assets, these happy memories also were kept alive as possessions reflecting the giver.

God, help us to face honestly the facts of death and try to prepare a worthy testament expressing loving concern.

NOVEMBER 9. *And she said, As the Lord thy God liveth, I have not a cake, but an handful of meal in a barrel, and a little oil in a cruse.*—I KINGS 17:12

As the holidays approach, the time comes to take stock of financial assets, and those of the mind and heart. We need to know what is available for entertaining and for gifts, and if we do not have ready the cake, we can at least be sure of our available assets, as was this thrifty woman of the scripture. Learning how to use simple substances to produce pleasure for strangers, family, and friends is one of the joys of living, and each fall there is fresh opportunity.

Father, we offer that which we do have into thy keeping, asking thee to give us wisdom in using talents and money happily.

NOVEMBER 10. *Say not thou, I will recompense evil; but wait on the Lord, and he shall save thee.—* PROVERBS 20:22

Bad debts, whether they be financial or those involved with personalities and heartache, have a way of coming due for collection. The individual who says arrogantly that he will recompense evil, or who repays grudgingly, or who goes out of his way to be vengeful in dealing with one who has harmed him in the past, is only asking for more trouble. There is a better way out for the payment of bad debts, and that is to wait patiently on God in prayer, asking for funds and forgiveness. Such practical aspects of living are rightful prayer requests.

Father, when we are worried about finances keep us safe in thy care because we trust in thy answers.

NOVEMBER 11. *I will call on the Lord, who is worthy to be praised: so shall I be saved from mine enemies.*—II SAMUEL 22:4

In this famous passage of a song by David, there is the universal hope of hearts to be saved from enemies and to give thanks to God for victory. Sometimes this praise must be given through tears, as families recall the great and terrible sacrifices of their fathers, sons, and brothers. This loss is compounded when victory seems to be taken for granted by those who have not made sacrifices of substance. Calling upon God for comfort and peace remains the way to personal victory over sorrow and suffering.

God, accept our deep gratitude for those who have loved us with their very lives, and make us worthy citizens.

NOVEMBER 12. *Mine eye also is dim by reason of sorrow, and all my members are as a shadow.*—JOB 17:7

On the day after any national holiday, there is often an aftermath which calls for courage. Others may forget the mourning for a lost soldier, but the heart most intimately concerned finds the return to the workaday world almost more than can be faced. There may be a fresh traffic statistic because of an automobile accident on what was meant to be a carefree day. It is normal and human to weep for our sorrows, but always the way of courage beckons ahead with comfort and peace.

Father, our humanity often obscures our vision of thee, which we would have restored and renewed with greater clarity.

NOVEMBER 13. *Give her of the fruit of her hands; and let her own works praise her in the gates.*—Proverbs 31:31

Work is a precious antidote for sorrow or depression, and the effects of work in the garden are readily seen in the harvest month of November. Ripened plums, ready for jelly in the glass, or falling nuts to be shelled and covered with a sugary mint sauce, speak of the work of the hands in the garden. Such delicacies, when prepared in the kitchen, bespeak the special skills of the housewife and are enjoyed by family and friends alike. Such gifts of working hands bless those who give and receive.

God, we would keep our hands busy at tasks, fitting us for the harvest of life when our earthly days are finished.

NOVEMBER 14. *But when the blade was sprung up, and brought forth fruit, then appeared the tares also.*—Matthew 13:26

Weeds are plainly visible in the month of harvest—the natural outgrowth of the tares, about which Jesus spoke to his disciples in a memorable parable. Sometimes it seems today that evil pops up whenever an effort is made to do a good deed or begin a constructive project. The weeds of discontent and destruction grow alongside the efforts to help and be constructive. This contrast calls for dedicated men and women who will place themselves on the side of those who would bring forth good fruit.

Father, forgive us if we have helped the tares of this life, and help us learn how to grow and produce for thee.

NOVEMBER 15. *For thou art my lamp, O Lord: and the Lord will lighten my darkness.*—II SAMUEL 22:29

Each evening in November it becomes expedient to light the lamps a little earlier, as darkness falls on the earth. A brilliant sunset may glow into the living room reminding us that the lights should come on for the reading of the evening paper. We have ways to deal with darkness in the modern world of conveniences and equipment. Yet in the darkness of the heart there remains the one tried and true method which has been available since Old Testament times—trust in the Lord.

Lord, we accept the light of thy love anew, for we need fresh portions of it in the darkness of modern cruelties.

NOVEMBER 16. *So shall my word be that goeth forth out of my mouth: it shall not return unto me void, but it shall accomplish that which I please, and it shall prosper in the thing whereto I sent it.*—ISAIAH 55:11

This beloved verse of prophecy refers to seedtime and harvest, which is so abundantly visible during the month of November. In many ways this is a most reassuring time, in that it makes clear the truths about spiritual harvests as well as the natural ripening of the grain in the fields. How wonderful to know that God's word is destined to prosper, leading to the time of eternal everlasting harvest.

Father, when we are tempted to be discouraged by the transient evidences of evil, help us to remember thy never-failing prophecies.

NOVEMBER 17. *For they have sown the wind, and they shall reap the whirlwind.*—HOSEA 8:7

Howling around the corners of the house, the wind sweeps across the earth in November, sometimes delaying the huge ships of the sky as well as the sea. This powerful force is often forgotten in the even tenor of good days, but when fall winds blow in full force it is easy to see their intensity. Spiritual whirlwinds also gather force from small beginnings in acceptance of easy temptations to laziness or sloth.

Father, keep us diligently working for good, so that evil winds of destruction will not assail our spirits.

211

NOVEMBER 18. *They helped every one his neighbour; and every one said to his brother, Be of good courage.*—ISAIAH 41:6

In pioneer days it used to be the custom for neighbors to help each other with the harvesting, doing the actual work in the fields. As the country became more urban, with large cities as well as farms, some of this neighborliness was lost. It may not be practical any longer to share the work of hands in these days of big harvesting machines, but it is always desirable to help neighbors with cheerful words of encouragement.

Father, give us helpful words in time of need, and cheerful hearts always to face whatever the day may bring.

NOVEMBER 19. *Great peace have they which love thy law: and nothing shall offend them.*—PSALM 119:165

Moments of peace are rare in the world because of wars and rumors of wars, so the peaceful sight of a sunny clear day in November is especially welcomed. Perhaps this is a fresh Sabbath morning as the family starts for church, or a crisp starlit evening as friends say good night after dinner together. Such human moments of peace are to be cherished, and all of them are enhanced by the inner peace of the person who is aware of the precious promises of God for lasting peace.

God, we would identify with causes for peace, contributing our small share to total peace for thy beautiful world.

NOVEMBER 20. *O give thanks unto the Lord; call upon his name: make known his deeds among the people.*—PSALM 105:1

A high point in November is the observance of Thanksgiving Day, begun in America, and now stretching around the world through the efforts of young servicemen and women to keep alive a happy tradition of home. The tempting, luscious turkey cooked in the family kitchen has its counterpart in imitation dinners, perhaps made from canned meats or native chickens. What matters is the spirit of thankfulness for the blessings of food and fellowship. Thankfulness is a way to bless the name of God.

God, forgive us for taking for granted so much of thy bounty, and keep alive in our hearts the spirit of Thanksgiving Day.

NOVEMBER 21. *The Lord is good unto them that wait for him, to the soul that seeketh him.*—LAMENTATIONS 3:25

Waiting is never easy, even if it is just that moment before the cutting of the pumpkin pie when the smallest member of the family wiggles in his seat and puts out a finger to touch the whipped cream. But even restless waiting is better than turning away in disappointment or anger or disgust. Continually the Bible points out the necessity to keep on seeking God and answers to personal problems. Many can testify to the importance of just waiting a little longer.

God, help us to cling to that powerful word "wait," knowing that good action results from true seeking and patient waiting.

NOVEMBER 22. *But now our soul is dried away: there is nothing at all, beside this manna, before our eyes.* —NUMBERS 11:6

After the joy of a Thanksgiving feast, it is hard to come down to the leftovers and then return to everyday menus. Complaints sometimes come from the one who must do the daily cooking as well as the family which wants something different. This attitude can turn the best meal into a disaster. Grumbling seems to be a natural quality. Even those who had been saved by God's daily manna murmured against it, and we often are as ungrateful for daily blessings of food and shelter.

God, keep us from having monotonous souls, chanting a singsong of complaints while we have the choice of words of thanks.

NOVEMBER 23. *But I was an herdman, and a gatherer of sycamore fruit.*—AMOS 7:14

As sheep and cattle go into winter pasture the herdsman has his place even in contemporary life. Such men have many modest characteristics. Here the prophet gives humble testimony of his work, expressing one of the greatest attributes of true thanksgiving. When we realize that it is God who gives to us the power to succeed at our tasks, we are in a position to act with thankfulness and grow into greater service.

Father, with this prophet of old we would remember our own fields of service and ask thy continuing grace.

NOVEMBER 24. *To him the porter openeth; and the sheep hear his voice: and he calleth his own sheep by name, and leadeth them out.*—JOHN 10:3

The work of a porter is important, whether it involves sheep in the pasture, or the shepherding of a large flock of tourists into a hotel room with all their luggage. Much confusion can be avoided when sheep or people truly know the voice of the one in charge. This is what makes for right living in confused days, also, for it is increasingly necessary to listen for the voice of God offering guidance to his children.

God, in the machine age we forget that thou dost call us by name, and we want to be led by thee.

NOVEMBER 25. *Ye observe days, and months, and times, and years.*—GALATIANS 4:10

Glancing at the calendar on this day in November, sometimes a housewife will exclaim, "One month from today is actually Christmas Day." Every year the day seems to come a little more quickly than in the previous year, and always there are many tasks to be accomplished. It is true that, even as the New Testament says, we do observe many days; but when the heart is prepared with thanksgiving, all such occasions have lasting fellowship and charm.

Father, with gratitude for thy goodness we look forward to the forthcoming events of significant fellowship.

NOVEMBER 26. *And she said, I will surely go with thee.*—JUDGES 4:9

As holiday lists are prepared, it is good to be able to go to the telephone and ask a friend to join in a shopping expedition, perhaps the sales after Thanksgiving Day which many stores hold currently. How wonderful it is to have a friend who can be counted upon surely to share such casual events, but who is also available if there is a needed trip to the hospital or a lawyer's office. Even more heartwarming is the assurance of the comforting presence of the spirit of God in daily living.

God, make us more faithful friends ourselves, so that we may contribute steadfastness to those who need our presence.

NOVEMBER 27. *Who shall separate us from the love of Christ?*—ROMANS 8:35

When a child becomes separated from his mother in a shopping crowd, it is a fearsome time for both of them. Often the loudspeaker in the large department store will call out the information that there is a "lost parent," and a "found child" to be claimed at the information desk, hoping by this light approach to relieve the tension caused by being separated from loved ones. Something great and overwhelming happens in the life joined to God and freed from the fear of separation.

God, if we have permitted attitudes to separate us from thee, remove these impediments now and restore us fully.

NOVEMBER 28. *In his humiliation his judgment was taken away.*—ACTS 8:33

To be humiliated before friends or family is a tragic experience. The offices of many medical doctors and psychologists are filled these days with people whose problems stem from such treatment. Humiliation often leads to quick actions taken in revenge or anger, and thus the problem is made greater. Burdens caused by humiliation should be thrown away in fall before the happiest season of the year, so that the soul need carry no excess baggage of sorrow.

God, even as the autumn leaves fly away from the trees, take our moments of humiliation away and restore judgment.

NOVEMBER 29. *Be sober, be vigilant; because your adversary the devil, as a roaring lion, walketh about, seeking whom he may devour.*—I PETER 5:8

Children who hear the thunder and lightning of a November storm may think that the weather roars like a lion. They may even imitate his sounds as they crouch behind big chairs in "pretend" games while the rain continues outside. But the parents know that this play is possible because someone has been vigilant and seen to it that the roof has been repaired and that the windows are tightly latched against the wind and moisture. We are told to prepare our hearts in advance against the storms of evil.

Father, make us vigilant servants of thine, aware of the cracks in our spiritual houses before great damage ensues.

NOVEMBER 30. *For now we live, if ye stand fast in the Lord.*—I Thessalonians 3:8

With thankfulness to God for his blessings as expressed in Thanksgiving Day and the special observance of the sacrifices of veterans, we realize that the month of November makes a real impact on the heart. In an election year there is both disappointment when a favorite candidate fails to win, and the need to rally behind whomever is chosen as leader. An awareness of citizenship and what it has cost in lives brings gratitude for liberty and a fresh knowledge of the importance of an active faith in service.

God, help us gather our spiritual forces together that we may truly serve thee in our age and generation with thanksgiving.

December

KING OF OUR LIVES, WE ACKNOWL-
EDGE ANEW THY RIGHTFUL PLACE IN
OUR DAILY ACTIVITIES. ENLARGE OUR
HEARTS TO NEW TRUST BY DRAW-
ING US ALL WITHIN THE LOVING
CIRCLE OF CHRISTMAS.

DECEMBER 1. *I will greatly rejoice in the Lord, my soul shall be joyful in my God.*—ISAIAH 61:10

On the first day in December, many children start count-ing off the days until Christmas, while adults often add to the long list of things to do in this busy month. Whether the mood is anticipation of the day, or participa-tion in activities leading up to it, the underlying feeling should be one of joyful preparation. Putting joy into the month of December can have its carry-over value in all the year to follow.

God, give us joyous hearts to increase our energy for chores involving our loved ones and in serving thee.

DECEMBER 2. *I will instruct thee and teach thee in the way which thou shalt go: I will guide thee with mine eye.*—PSALM 32:8

A wise friend confided, "Each Christmas I learn something new by reading the advertisements. They teach me what has been developed in the way of unusual toys and good things to eat." There is wisdom in continuing to learn about this interesting world in which we live, and none of us ever gets beyond the need of instruction. Often it is hard to accept when the way of life seems to teach us that we need to go in another direction than we had intended, but this way may have new opportunities.

God, we need to be taught the joy of daily blessings, and we do ask thee to keep us aware of thy goodness always.

DECEMBER 3. *But let patience have her perfect work, that ye may be perfect and entire, wanting nothing.*—JAMES 1:4

Often it seems as if December is a "month of wants," as each child writes down his hopes for certain presents. Even the various church and community agencies express their wishes for little red wagons, new clothing for minority groups, or homemade cookies for nursing homes where the aged live out their days. Listening and meeting various demands calls for patience in busy lives. Cultivating of patience is one of the best gifts life gives to seeking hearts, for it leads to peace.

Father, take away our impatient natures so that we may see that we do want for nothing while we trust in thee.

DECEMBER 4. *Now God himself and our Father, and our Lord Jesus Christ, direct our way unto you.* —I Thessalonians 3:11

Sitting down to address the first Christmas cards of the year, one often longs to be able to visit in person with old friends and neighbors. Even in the act of directing a card with the address there is a moment of deep nostalgia, and a realization that yet another year has gone by without the achievement of a visit with one who may live comparatively nearby and close at hand. Then the knowledge that we are linked together in God and enjoy his fellowship is reassuring.

God, help us to grow in grace and toward thee so that we may feel at one in spirit with others who share this fellowship.

DECEMBER 5. *And the taste of it was like wafers made with honey.*—EXODUS 16:31

One of the joys of this month is looking at the colored pages of illustrated recipes in the women's magazines. Sometimes they seem to make the mouth water as luscious phrases describe the delicious foods. Certainly a wonderful phrase is that which tells of the manna which God provided for his children. Today's verse not only suggests a taste, but sends the fragrance of the honey across the years. God's provisions are sweet and meet the needs of body and heart.

God, for daily manna in the space age, we are grateful as we think of new uses of thy abundant provisions.

DECEMBER 6. *That they do good, that they be rich in good works, ready to distribute, willing to communicate.*—I TIMOTHY 6:18

This description of ideal conduct sent to the early Christians seems an apt summary of what people today have stored up for them in the holiday month. Increasingly we need to communicate with friends through seasonal letters, take clothing to the community agencies which distribute it to the needy, and carry through good ideas into good works. Happy is the heart which has learned to translate this verse into modern action.

223

Father, we are glad that the Bible sums up for us high ideals of conduct to use as goals for daily living.

DECEMBER 7.   *Even in laughter the heart is sorrowful; and the end of that mirth is heaviness.*—Proverbs 14:13

When happy days of rejoicing come near a time of great national sorrow, there is always a combination of emotions. Some veterans lingering in hospitals following the sacrifices made necessary by Pearl Harbor still find the holiday season one of continual physical suffering. Many families mourn the loss of loved ones and see younger sons now involved with other military activities. Preparation for Christmas calls for remembrance of those who serve their country, and the comforting of those long involved with sorrow.

God, keep us from being thoughtless and selfish by our forgetfulness of those whose service blesses our country.

DECEMBER 8.   *I will walk before the Lord in the land of the living.*—Psalm 116:9

A choice faces each person preparing for the holidays. The heart can live on nostalgic memories of the past, or awaken to future opportunities for pleasures and fellowship. If the year has called for the loss of loved ones, then the determination has to be made by an act of will that the walk to this holiday will be made with the living, whose interests must be kept in mind and not pulled back into sadness. God can grant the necessary strength to turn the mind forward.

Father, comfort us as we leave the past behind, and help us to be more compassionate toward those fighting grief.

DECEMBER 9. *A time to rend, and a time to sew; a time to keep silence, and a time to speak.*—ECCLESIASTES 3:7

As the year is in its last month, an abundance of special "times" is presented, with many activities which need to be done in small or large groups. Sometimes two or three women meet together to sew red tarlatan socks to be filled with candies as a treat for children at a holiday party. They speak of those who need to be remembered, and recall in silent fellowship the happy memories of those who served in other years. December can be a fulfilling time of active service for all.

Father, in the variety of activities available to each of us, help us to find thee ever closer and dearer to our hearts.

DECEMBER 10. *And I made treasurers over the treasuries.*—NEHEMIAH 13:13

Money and its attendant problems are a normal part of December. Way back in Old Testament times it was necessary to appoint people to be "treasurers over the treasuries." This mouth-filling phrase describes the faithful men and women today who count the weekly offerings in Sunday schools and take them to the banks on Monday mornings to be deposited. Such service is often unhonored, but how important it is when funds are needed for literature to study, or costumes for the Christmas pageant. Wise keeping of money is an honorable trust.

God, help us to watch our own purses and commit our funds to thee that we may be guided in both saving and spending.

DECEMBER 11. *These words spake Jesus in the treasury, as he taught in the temple.*—JOHN 8:20

This explanatory phrase follows beautiful statements of Jesus and links the treasury with the temple itself, something we sometimes hesitate to do in modern times. Our money is considered separately from our worship until some special occasion calls for a certain offering. In the month of Christmas, we have opportunity to become aware that our sharing of substance can be a year round act of worship, if we channel a portion of our wages into missionary activities. The beautiful services of Advent only focus attention on far-reaching yearly needs.

Father, as Christmas makes us more generous in our hearts, give us the joy of growth into new standards of giving for thee.

DECEMBER 12. *But be ye doers of the word, and not hearers only, deceiving your own selves.*—JAMES 1:22

Hearing music is one of the great pleasures of the month of December. Church choirs and community choruses present programs for which the preparation may have consumed many months of practice time. As the "Hallelujah Chorus" resounds through magnificent auditoriums with stained-glass windows, or is repeated in tiny white churches over record players, the heart responds with its own "Amen." The Bible says that those who hear must also do, or else their idealism becomes deceitful.

Lord, love us into action, prompted by the beautiful harmonious strains of music honoring thee.

DECEMBER 13. *Better is it that thou shouldest not vow, than that thou shouldest vow and not pay.*—Ec-CLESIASTES 5:5.

Promises made to children must be kept at all costs, a prominent psychologist advises in dealing with disturbed situations. Therefore it becomes of great importance to keep from promising gifts or actions which cannot be fulfilled within the family budget. We see new items and long to possess them, without truly understanding the cost. This is sometimes true of such virtues as graciousness and kindness which we covet in others, but are not willing to pay the price in controlling tactless tongues or ridicule. Our vows to become better may be honored in Christmas sharing.

God, we know that thou dost keep thy promises and we rely on them, as we ask for help to fulfill our best vows.

DECEMBER 14. *Then the king commanded to call the magicians, and the astrologers, and the sorcerers.* —DANIEL 2:2

A happy tradition of the Christmastide in many lands is the showing of tricks of magic to children whose laughter can be heard throughout the room where the entertainment is held. All of us have something of this childlike wish to be entertained by magic, and the holidays present an opportunity for festivities which lighten the year's burdens and daily plodding. December also offers an opportunity for the most wonderful magic of all—that of the heart which changes on contact with spiritual ideals and a fresh view of God's love.

Father, work thy eternal magic in our hearts, that we may be changed into the persons thou dost mean for us to be always.

DECEMBER 15. *But the word is very nigh unto thee, in thy mouth, and in thy heart, that thou mayest do it.* —DEUTERONOMY 30:14

Decorations on the tops of store buildings as well as in the windows, showing the shepherds tending their flocks and the tiny babe asleep in the cradle testify to the word of Christmas made manifest in modern industry. Carols which come from the radio into grocery stores with their foods for baking Christmas cookies tell the age-old story. Indeed the word is "nigh thee" in the modern age, from all sides, to be received into the heart and acted upon and not scorned as merely ordinary commercialism. There is joy in daily appreciation.

Father, deliver us from sophistication and shallowness, and let us hear the sacred story anew.

DECEMBER 16. *He discovereth deep things out of darkness, and bringeth out to light the shadow of death.* —JOB 12:22

Each day it gets dark a little earlier in the first part of December. Sometimes it is necessary to light the lamps almost in midafternoon on a cloudy day. In such a month of short days and long nights of darkness comes the happy feast of Christmas, which calls for lights around the family dinner table and getting out the candles to place in the windows. All such symbols of light emphasize the eternal light which came into the world on the first precious Christmas Day.

Father, help us to remove darkness out of our hearts, that the light of Christmas may reflect into all portions of our lives.

DECEMBER 17. *Let your light so shine before men, that they may see your good works, and glorify your Father which is in heaven.* —Matthew 5:16

Lighting a silver candle in front of the blue wreath to form an attractive centerpiece for a Christmas party may add the final touch of perfection to a beautiful celebration, planned to the last detail. So it is that the many trivial activities of Christmas shopping and baking should be brought together until they make a light of fellowship before friends and family which will truly illuminate the home, and show the love of God expressed through Christmas.

Father, help us to know deep within us that we are a part of the great light of Christmas in this modern age.

DECEMBER 18. *The works of his hands are verity and judgment; all his commandments are sure.*—Psalm 111:7

One of the joys of the week before Christmas is putting final touches on gifts. Children home from school on vacation look to this as a time of making something— perhaps a bookmark from a piece of red satin ribbon with a snapshot pasted on, showing grandfather fishing with the child who is making the gift. All these loving touches made by young hands and old link the heart to God, whose hands hold truth and justice, and whose commandments make for wholesome living.

God, give us this sense of divine fellowship with thee, as our hands keep busy on projects for those we love.

DECEMBER 19. *If so be ye have tasted that the Lord is gracious.*—I Peter 2:3

231

Glibly we speak of "taste treats" in the holiday season. In some communities groups of young mothers get together for a cookie exchange, each bringing a plate of her favorite recipe and offering one tidbit with the recipe to each of the friends present, who in turn contributes a recipe and a sample snack. In such tasting there is testing of the product. Each of us has the same right and privilege to test the gracious love of God in our lives when we ask for guidance.

Father, may this Christmastime bring a fresh reminder that we may always taste and see that the Lord is good.

DECEMBER 20. *The spirit of man is the candle of the Lord.*—PROVERBS 20:27

Making of varicolored candles is one of the fascinating projects of the modern holiday season. Old candles of many colors are converted into new shapes by pouring the liquid wax into holders in flower shapes or cut from milk cartons. Whatever the shape, the light is as old as mankind, and the flickering candle links the modern generation to the earliest settlers. So God's eternal light is reflected in the spirit of man and should be kept pure and beautiful in loving action.

Lord of light, help us to lift our hearts to thee when our lamps grow dim, that we may receive new lustre.

DECEMBER 21. *And let us consider one another to provoke unto love and to good works.*—HEBREWS 10:24

When the little girl reached for the white tissue paper, her arm struck the ball of red ribbon, which unwound as it hit the floor. Trying to find the loose end, her mother spoke sharply, and the child ran from the room in tears. Wisely the mother went after her and said, "I must be real tired or I wouldn't get provoked so easily. Please come back and help me." Soon they were happily finishing the loving Christmas wrappings.

God, take away any sense of strain and stress at this season, and let our lives be provoked only to pursue peace.

DECEMBER 22. *Freely ye have received, freely give.*—MATTHEW 10:8

A simple phrase like this is often quoted as a maxim, but the reason such mottoes become threadbare and overworked is that their truth is needed anew in each generation. True gifts come from the knowledge that we have been given much in the way of blessings, often intangible but providing the background for tangible positions and worth. Surface gifts serve best when they are based on the knowledge of inner gifts received from life through God's abundance.

Father, keep us from being misers in the sharing of such gifts as love, appreciation, encouragement, and confidence.

DECEMBER 23. *Nevertheless he left not himself without witness . . . filling our hearts with food and gladness.*—ACTS 14:17

Season of "food and gladness" is the Christmastime, with this mood increasing as the great day draws nearer. Giggles of small children hiding presents under the bed or back in a desk drawer vie with the sounds of the pots and pans in the kitchen being moved to make way for the extra provisions for the dinner to be served day after tomorrow. These earthly chores are a part of the preparation for the observance of the celebrated fact that God did send his "witness" into the world. This central point blesses all Christmas activities.

God, may we witness for thee in our happy acceptance of the special gladness that is inherent in Christmas projects.

DECEMBER 24. *And God made two great lights; . . . he made the stars also.*—GENESIS 1:16

Christmas Eve is the time for caroling, singing again the age-old carols of love and peace and goodwill. Then, if ever, the eyes are aware of the stars in God's sky, which shine over his earth through all the nights of the year, whether they are hidden because of clouds or storms or are plainly visible in a clear, cloudless evening. The stars are faithful in their courses, a reminder of the beautiful unchanging laws of God manifest for his children.

God, for the joys of Christmas Eve fellowship under the stars, hear our carols of harmony and bless our lips.

DECEMBER 25. *But when the fulness of the time was come, God sent forth his Son, made of a woman, made under the law.*—GALATIANS 4:4

Even as tiny children wait with great anticipation for the coming of Christmas morning, so the world had been waiting for many centuries for the appearance of the Saviour. He did not appear until "the fulness of the time" according to the Bible story. In this fact there is great and abiding comfort for all who wait for loved ones to accept a Saviour, or for the coming of some cherished dream which seems long delayed. The great gift of Christmas is the promise of God's love revealed at the proper time.

Father, we accept the promises of Christmas, and ask thee to make them realities in our hearts and lives.

DECEMBER 26. *He shall glorify me: for he shall receive of mine, and shall shew it unto you.*—JOHN 16:14

If Christmas is considered as a golden coin, there are two sides neatly joined together, those of giving and receiving. While it is important to learn how to give graciously, there is also an art to receiving with grace and joy. Even as children like to display their toys on the morning after Christmas, the disciples of Jesus are to show the evidences of their new state of mind and heart in witnessing to others.

God of Christmas morning, help us to keep thy eternal gifts in circulation as we meet with others who need thy love.

DECEMBER 27. *For so an entrance shall be ministered unto you abundantly into the everlasting kingdom of our Lord and Saviour Jesus Christ.*—II PETER 1:11

In the week between Christmas and New Year's Day, there is the happy custom of "Open House" involving neighbors and friends. Sometimes it is a once a year enjoyment, participated in by relatives who drive considerable distances. With the entry way decorated with an attractive wreath and the door opened with a smile and handshake of welcome, this is a moment which promises wonderful fellowship. It is a time to greet also the new neighbor and foreign student.

Father, keep us from selfish enjoyment of the familiar without opening the door wider into areas of Christian fellowship.

DECEMBER 28. *And the barbarous people shewed us no little kindness: for they kindled a fire, and received us every one.*—ACTS 28:2

What joy there is in warming the hands before an open fire and finding heartwarming fellowship with friends in the circle. There is something especially joyous about the fragrant fire at Christmastime, perhaps with some of the boughs of greenery from over the mantel included in the flames, or the little sprays of cedar and fir which graced the packages. In times of loneliness at the holidays or thinking of the end of the year, the word of God can provide this warming fire for the heart grown cold.

Father, for the remembered beauty of faces of loved ones reflected in the Christmas firelight, accept our thanks.

DECEMBER 29. *When I was a child, I spake as a child, I understood as a child, I thought as a child: but when I became a man, I put away childish things.* —I CORINTHIANS 13:11

Trying to persuade a child to put away his Christmas gifts is a hard job, particularly if the parent wants the youngster to write a thank-you note to the grandparents who sent the red sweater or talking doll. It is never easy at any age to put away the gifts which have been enjoyed in happy times, and to turn to the serious business of living or making new choices. Yet this is the mark of maturity, and after the happy nostalgic Christmas season a new year beckons ahead.

God, if there are happy and sad memories we should put away into thy safekeeping, give us the maturity to do this now.

DECEMBER 30. *And I thank Christ Jesus our Lord, who hath enabled me, for that he counted me faithful, putting me into the ministry.*—I TIMOTHY 1:12

Counting is a real chore at the end of the business year, many firms choosing this time for inventory. Individuals also have opportunity to take inventory of their assets and liabilities, good habits and bad, which make the balance sheet of the business of living. Happy is the heart which can say with this Bible verse that through the grace of God, the soul can be counted as faithful. Each of us has a different ministry of service to which God calls us daily.

238

Lord, let our lives reflect thy goodness, as we long to be counted in thy eternal kingdom.

DECEMBER 31. *I am Alpha and Omega, the beginning and the end, the first and the last.*—REVELATION 22:13

A common remark at all ages is the wistful statement, "If I could only know how it would all come out in the end." With this knowledge, we might plan differently, or take another route, or just relax in the one which seems most ordinary and comfortable. It is not ours to know the ending from the beginning, but we do have the great privilege of trusting the God who was in the beginning and who is also in the ending, and who invites us to join him in this great and wonderful enduring pilgrimage.

Dear God, we offer up the daily tasks of our earthly lives to thee and ask for thy blessing as one year ends and another begins.